# A Fine Bright Day Today

A play

Philip Goulding

Samuel French — London
www.samuelfrench-london.co.uk

Copyright © 2013 by Philip Goulding
All Rights Reserved

*A FINE BRIGHT DAY TODAY* is fully protected under the copyright laws of the British Commonwealth, including Canada, the United States of America, and all other countries of the Copyright Union. All rights, including professional and amateur stage productions, recitation, lecturing, public reading, motion picture, radio broadcasting, television and the rights of translation into foreign languages are strictly reserved.

ISBN 978-0-573-11132-7

www.samuelfrench.co.uk
www.samuelfrench.com

---

### For Amateur Production Enquiries

#### United Kingdom and World excluding North America

plays@samuelfrench.co.uk

020 7255 4302/01

Each title is subject to availability from Samuel French, depending upon country of performance.

---

CAUTION: Professional and amateur producers are hereby warned that *A FINE BRIGHT DAY TODAY* is subject to a licensing fee. Publication of this play does not imply availability for performance. Both amateurs and professionals considering a production are strongly advised to apply to the appropriate agent before starting rehearsals, advertising, or booking a theatre. A licensing fee must be paid whether the title is presented for charity or gain and whether or not admission is charged.

The Professional rights in this play are controlled by Eric Glass Ltd, 25 Ladbrooke Crescent, London W11 1PS.

No one shall make any changes in this title for the purpose of production. No part of this book may be reproduced, stored in a retrieval system, or transmitted in any form, by any means, now known or yet to be invented, including mechanical, electronic, photocopying, recording, videotaping, or otherwise, without the prior written permission of the publisher. No one shall upload this title, or part of this title, to any social media websites.

The right of Philip Goulding to be identified as author of this work has been asserted in accordance with Section 77 of the Copyright, Designs and Patents Act 1988.

## A FINE BRIGHT DAY TODAY

First presented at the Oldham Coliseum Theatre in June 2011 with the following cast:

**Margaret**                                              Christine Cox
**Rebecca**                                         Samantha Power
**Milton**                                              Robin Bowerman

Directed by Kevin Shaw
Designed by Alison Heffernan
Lighting designed by Jane Barrek
Sound designed by Lorna Munden
Original music by Alan Edward Williams

Subsequently presented at the New Vic Theatre, Newcastle-Under-Lyme in July 2012 with the following cast:

**Margaret**                                             Janine Birkett
**Rebecca**                                         Hayley Doherty
**Milton**                                                  Hugh Simon

Directed by Peter Leslie Wild
Designed by Libby Watson
Lighting designed by Daniella Beattie
Sound designed by James Earls-Davis
Original music by James Earls-Davis with Sue Moffat

# CHARACTERS

**Margaret Harvey**, 50s.
**Rebecca Harvey**, her daughter, 30s.
**Milton Farnsworth**, American, 60s.

## SYNOPSIS OF SCENES

The action of the play takes place in Margaret's kitchen, the yard outside her home and a nearby coastal path, in a British coastal town.

ACT I
SCENE 1  Margaret's kitchen. Autumn, late afternoon
SCENE 2  The same. A few days later, evening
SCENE 3  The same. A few days later, dusk
SCENE 4  The same. A few days later, late evening
SCENE 5  The same. Early the next morning
SCENE 6  The coastal path. A few days later, afternoon
SCENE 7  Margaret's kitchen. The evening of the same day

ACT II
SCENE 1  The yard. The next morning
SCENE 2  The coastal path. A week later, midday
SCENE 3  Margaret's kitchen. A few days later, night
SCENE 4  The coastal path. A few days later
SCENE 5  Margaret's kitchen. A few days later, morning
SCENE 6  The same. A week later, late at night
SCENE 7  Later the same night
SCENE 8  A moment later

Time — the present

Blackouts between scenes should be kept as brief as possible and the design should allow for fluidity of movement from one scene to the next.

# PRODUCTION NOTES

**Scene Changes**

In the New Vic Theatre, Newcastle-under-Lyme production, the scenes were set by the actors. Director Peter Leslie Wild's philosophy is that it's not about what moves where, or even who moves it — it's more to do with the story being told. Margaret tidying things away — or unplugging things before she goes out to work. Margaret watching Milton as he puts his bags in that same place on the stage for the last time. Milton handing the key back to Rebecca in exactly the same place she gave it to him at the beginning. Milton holding the chair for Margaret when they sit down for that first meal. What moves where and how obviously depends on the shape of the stage and what props the director deems necessary. Wild confessed he suffers from what he calls "empty stage phobia" and hates the idea of people in black scurrying around pretending not to be there. His belief is that a languid scene change that is interesting will always feel shorter than a rushed one that is uninteresting. The trick is to keep the audience involved for every second.

**Props**

It is preferable if the oven and toaster are actually operational, so that the scrambled eggs and toast can be created live on stage. This may make timings tricky — but it's good when it works.

**Music**

The first two productions of the play used specially commissioned music. At Oldham Coliseum Theatre Alan Edward Williams composed and recorded music for cello and piano. For the New Vic Theatre, Newcastle-under-Lyme, James Earls-Davis composed and recorded (with Sue Moffat) music for guitar and violin. If commissioned music is not an option then extant music can be used. But it should always be instrumental rather than vocal — and the music chosen should be appropriate to the emotion of the section of the play it is preceding, following or bridging.

**Philip Goulding**

Please see notice on p. 58 regarding the use of copyright music in performance.

## ACKNOWLEDGMENTS

Thanks to: Richard Annis, Frank Broom, Ian Butler, Ivan Cutting, Maggie Dooley, Mary Elliott Nelson, Rebecca Farrar, Isabel Ford, Steve Hall, Jeanette Hardiman, Theresa Heskins, Anne-Louise Jones, Maureen Kent, Natasha Kent, Mick Martin, Brian Morton, Burt Shavitz, Carl Shavitz, Alec Taylor, Kenneth Alan Taylor, Liz Wilson, Peter Wilson.

Other plays by Philip Goulding
published by Samuel French Ltd:

The Titfield Thunderbolt

# ACT I

## Scene 1

*Margaret's kitchen. Autumn, late afternoon*

*Music*

*The main part of the set is the kitchen of a cottage. There is a large, old wooden table and a sideboard with a table lamp on it. Around the table are placed at least three chairs — these need not match. There is a sink, a fridge, a stove and cupboards etc. By the look of it, most of the fittings have not been modernized for over 30 years. Two doors lead off — one through to the front door. The other is the back door, which leads through to the yard, the shed and the drive. The back door is the most in use. There is a mirror and a coat-stand near the front door. We can see some stairs disappearing off up to the next floor*

*To each side of the main area there are two other playing areas. One area represents the backyard/garden of the cottage. The other spreads across the far downstage area. This represents the cliff-path a few miles from the house. This area overlooks the sea*

*Margaret Harvey — a woman in her 50s — sits at the kitchen table. She is doing a crossword puzzle in the* Mail on Sunday. *There is a dictionary and an encyclopaedia within reach*

*Margaret gets up, scurries to the kitchen window and peeps out. A bump sounds from upstairs. Margaret hurries back to the table, leafs through a dictionary. There's the sound of someone coming downstairs*

*Rebecca Harvey, in her 30s, enters carrying a box of books etc. She stops, looks at Margaret for a moment, then carries the box out through the back door. Margaret looks up only when Rebecca has left the room*

*The music fades. The sound of seabirds. The Lights rise on Milton Farnsworth on the cliff path. Milton is in his 60s. He is American. He has a beard. He's dressed for outdoors: a high-end multi-pocket gilet/waistcoat, good-quality boots etc. He carries a small sketch book which he may occasionally doodle in. The music fades*

*Milton stares out to sea. He speaks to the audience*

**Milton**  The seascape painter Franklin Bowden Broome visited this coast in nineteen-o-nine and stayed 'til nineteen-eleven. During his time here he befriended — and made sketches of — a number of the local fisher folk. Some of these figures were later incorporated into his large-scale paintings. Though I am a great admirer of Franklin Bowden Broome, I possess neither his talent or his social acumen. In fact, I leave most social gatherings with the nagging sense that I've embarrassed myself in some unspecified way.

*Rebecca comes back into the kitchen*

**Margaret**  I suppose he's out there. Skulking in his pick-up truck.
**Rebecca**  Why ask? I imagine you'll have sneaked a look.

*Rebecca goes off upstairs*

**Margaret**  (*after her*) And he'll let you fetch and carry that heavy junk, I suppose.
**Rebecca**  (*off*) I'm fine.

*A jet-fighter is heard low overhead, hurtling past. Margaret looks up in annoyance*

*On the cliff-path Milton ducks in reaction to the low-flying jet-fighter. This annoys and embarrasses him. He straightens up, watches the plane disappear into the distance*

**Milton**  I am inextricably drawn to the sea. As it was for Bowden Broome, so it is for me. In his case, of course, it was what he *wished to escape* that led him here — more so than what he hoped to find. He'd become sought-after on the East Coast of America – a minor celebrity. But here, far from the clamour of local fame, he was left alone to enjoy the freedom of anonymity. As for myself, I photograph or sketch for the best part of the day, then — when evening falls — I "nurse a jar" in Ray's Bar and observe the natives at play.

*Rebecca comes through with another box*

**Margaret**  You'll wear those stairs out, the way you're going.
**Rebecca**  A lot of this stuff is thick with dust.
**Margaret**  You've long been old enough to keep your own cupboards clean.

Act I, Scene 1

*Rebecca goes out again through the back door*

**Rebecca** (*as she goes*) It was just an observation.

**Margaret** (*after her*) I'd not bite him, you know, if he was wanting to help.

**Milton** Although I've found them to be a reticent people in the main, a few of the locals like to talk. I'm a bit of an exotic, maybe. (*Pause*) But I don't confide much, never could. I might endeavour to be more ... *human*, I suppose — dredge up some scraps of personal cogitation to share with Ray. (*Pause*) They're fond of the weather here — I've noticed that. They like *talking* about the weather, is what I mean.

*Rebecca comes back in*

**Margaret** You picked a nice day for it at least.

*On her way through, Rebecca gets a biscuit from the biscuit jar – she does not replace the lid of the jar*

*Rebecca goes back upstairs*

**Milton** It's not a hugely entertaining topic, but it passes the time. And — as I come from a land where weather can be extreme — I've compiled and rehearsed a few anecdotes; so everybody's happy in the end. In fact — just yesterday — I think I made a friend.

*The Lights go down on Milton*

**Margaret** (*shouting towards the stairs*) I wonder what your father would have thought.

*Rebecca comes back down the stairs carrying a bin bag full of stuff*

**Rebecca** That'll do for now.

*Rebecca goes to the sink and washes her hands. Margaret continues to half-focus on her crossword through what follows*

**Margaret** I said "I wonder what your father ..."
**Rebecca** I heard. I imagine he'd be surprised to find I hadn't left before. I hope he'd be pleased. I like to think Dad would have been fond of Pete.
**Margaret** He had few friends, your father. He wasn't that sort of man.

**Rebecca**  Well, maybe he'd have made an exception in Pete's case. For my sake.
**Margaret**  He liked a drink with his workmates. But I'd not call workmates friends.
**Rebecca**  Look, Mum ... if you expect me to feel guilty, I won't. I'm thirty-one. I couldn't stay living here forever, it was starting to look sad. (*Silence*) I don't *want* us to do this on bad terms, Mum. It's not even your approval I'm after — just your *blessing*. It'd be nice if you had faith in my decision. I'm not *deserting* you, you know — I'll be less than two miles down the road ...
**Margaret**  I've no idea what you're talking about, love. I've sat here, I've not said a word.
**Rebecca**  Perhaps you just need time to get used to it. (*Pause*) It'll be a bit strange for a while, that's all. Like when I first went to school. (*Pause*) I know you still miss him, Mum — that's natural. I miss him too.
**Margaret**  You never knew him, really.
**Rebecca**  It's not *the same*, obviously. But I've always felt *the lack of him* — his absence.
**Margaret**  You shouldn't keep him waiting. He might start tooting.
**Rebecca**  He's not like that. As you'd know if you gave him half a chance.
**Margaret**  I've to get ready for work anyway. I'm on evenings all this week.

*Margaret gets up from the table, starts to get ready for work — going to fetch her coat, perhaps*

**Rebecca**  Fine. I'll come by later for the rest of my stuff.
**Margaret**  You've got your key.
**Rebecca**  Right. (*Pause*) Fine. Bye.

*Rebecca takes the bin bag and exits*

*Margaret looks after her, surprised by the suddenness of her going*

*The sound of the truck door slamming and the truck moving off*

*Margaret replaces the lid on the biscuit jar, unplugs the kettle etc. then exits*

*As the Lights go down on the kitchen. The lights come up on Milton on the cliff path*

Act I, Scene 2

**Milton**  What I eventually produce is never quite as I envisaged. Everyday I struggle with my own inadequacy. Why don't I paint something other than the sea — open myself up to other things? If I could *get it right* just once — perhaps ... But she's never still ... never the same. Always familiar, yet somehow strange. Then again: could be the sea is just the sea is just the sea. On my worst days, that's what I really think.

*Milton pulls a sweet bar out of one of his pockets, unwraps it and starts to eat with an urgency and no sense of pleasure*

*Music*

*Black-out*

Scene 2

*The same. A few days later. Evening*

*Music fades*

*We hear a pick-up truck draw up outside the house. Rebecca comes in the back door*

**Rebecca**  Mum? Mum!

*Rebecca notices a framed picture propped up on the kitchen table. She picks it up and looks at it. She smiles, then becomes more concerned. She takes care to replace the picture exactly where it was. She goes to the foot of the stairs*

Mum?

*Margaret enters from the yard, carrying a box of junk, which she places downstage*

There you are.

*Rebecca goes to Margaret and hugs her. It's a bit awkward; Margaret doesn't hug*

**Margaret**  What's this in aid of?

*Margaret starts busying herself sorting out the contents of the box*

**Rebecca**  Are you OK?
**Margaret**  You thought I'd pine away without you?
**Rebecca**  Of course not. I've been spending at least three nights a week over there for the past two years; it's not such a great upheaval.
**Margaret**  Well, you've your things now, at least.
**Rebecca**  It was mostly just junk, like you said. Stuff I hardly ever look at. Most of it's gone straight in the attic.
**Margaret**  It could have just as well stayed where it was. (*Pause*) I've been sorting through that clutter in the shed. Found that picture of your dad. You could find a place for it, perhaps. It's one he never saw. (*Pause*) I found this, too. (*She hands her a photograph*) You in that daft hat.
**Rebecca**  What a sight I look.
**Margaret**  You were mad about that hat.
**Rebecca**  Did people laugh?
**Margaret**  They found it endearing I think. A tad eccentric, maybe. You were a happy little soul. Always chatting on and making friends. (*Pointedly*) You were a lovely child.
**Rebecca**  (*sarcastically*) Thanks.

*Margaret puts the photo of Rebecca on the sideboard. Then she carries on going through the box. She finds an old candleholder, which she puts into a cupboard near the sink*

**Margaret**  You could make yourself a drink or something.
**Rebecca**  I'm OK. I'm cutting out caffeine on account of my heads. Pete's convinced that's what's to blame.
**Margaret**  It's more likely the beer.
**Rebecca**  He's had a poem accepted, by the way. It's for an anthology published by a small press.
**Margaret**  Will he get paid?
**Rebecca**  It's a nominal fee.
**Margaret**  What does that mean?
**Rebecca**  It's not about the money, it's more the prestige. Besides, he's making a bit from his creative writing classes; we don't go short. I could do with working less, if anything — I can't believe my caseload. We're the growth industry round here, social services. I'm being flippant.
**Margaret**  It's not much of a joke, love.

*Rebecca gets up, fetches a yoghurt from the fridge and begins to eat it*

Act I, Scene 2                                                                 7

*Margaret has found an envelope of photographs*

(*Reading the envelope*) "Blackpool nineteen-eighty." Ted and Gwen Davy. And little Neil. He'll have children of his own by now, probably. We lost touch. As the fishing went so many upped and moved away.

**Rebecca**  You could always try to find them. Some people spend half their lives online, seeking out old friends. If you wanted me to help, I can always ...

*Margaret maybe discovers a hideous old wall-plate in the box of stuff. Perhaps it's something Rebecca years ago insisted be removed from sight. Margaret places the wall-plate back on a hook on the wall*

**Margaret**  I'm not fussed, love. As we haven't kept in contact, I can't have meant that much to them.

**Rebecca**  Or they to you. (*Pause*) Still, you've got the girls at work.

**Margaret**  Oh, they look on me as some old relic. We don't socialize much, these days. A drink on someone's birthday, occasionally a show. I missed the last one though, I can't think why ...

**Rebecca**  It had that bloke off the telly in, the one you don't like.

**Margaret**  And I'm too old to be travelling all that way.

*Margaret might find an old vase in the box — which she puts on the sideboard*

**Rebecca**  You talk as if you're in your dotage! Oh, I meant to say — I got talking to this bloke down at Ray's. An American. He's staying at that skanky B&B down on Sea View Road. He was saying he could do with somewhere cleaner and quieter.

**Margaret**  What on earth's that got to do with me?

**Rebecca**  I couldn't get much sense out of him at first — he seemed obsessed with the weather. Turns out he's an artist — on the Bowden Broome trail. But he's respectable enough — wears one of those waistcoats with all the pockets. Anyway, we had a couple of pints and I told him you'd a room. He's out most of the day, wandering about – so he'd be no trouble. It wouldn't hurt to meet him, I thought.

*Margaret finds some old books at the bottom of the box, which she puts into the sideboard*

**Margaret**  I am *not* a rest-home, Rebecca, for sundry waifs and strays.

**Rebecca**  The extra income, too, would come in handy.

**Margaret**  You don't need to worry about me. I've one less mouth to feed, with you not being here.

**Rebecca**  I always paid my share.
**Margaret**  It was never asked for.
**Rebecca**  (*breezily*) Anyway, I told him to drop by one evening this week. (*She gets up and starts to go out*) Oh, I almost forgot, I've some flowers in the car — I thought they'd brighten the place up — I'll fetch them in. Oh ... (*She remembers the photograph of Dad*) Thanks for this, Mum.
**Margaret**  Rebecca ...?
**Rebecca**  What?
**Margaret**  If he does turn up, this *man*, what on earth am I supposed to say?
**Rebecca**  I wouldn't worry. Once he's met you, he's just as likely to decide he doesn't want to stay.

*Rebecca exits*

*Music*

*Black-out*

## Scene 3

*The same. A few days later. Dusk*

*The music fades. The sound of rain*

*There are flowers on the table or the sideboard. There is a banging on the front door. Margaret comes down the stairs carrying a bucket. She wears rubber gloves and an apron. Underneath the apron she's dressed slightly better than usual*

**Margaret**  Hold on!
**Milton**  (*off, knocking again*) Anyone about?! Mrs Harvey? It's Milton Farnsworth ...
**Margaret**  Just a minute!

*Margaret takes off her rubber gloves. She starts to go to the front door, then remembers she's wearing the apron. She removes it. Pauses briefly to look at herself in the mirror. Arranges her hair. Then opens the front door*

*A bedraggled Milton is standing there*

You're sopping wet.

Act I, Scene 3                                                                9

**Milton**  Yup. I'm kind of aware of that.
**Margaret**  Come in. Wait there.
**Milton**  Your outside light, by the way, doesn't appear to be working.
**Margaret**  It works fine. I'm just not outside.

*Margaret comes back through to the kitchen, grabs a pile of old newspapers*

**Milton**  Right ... I'll leave my coat and boots here, shall I? (*He starts removing his hat, coat and boots*; *answering his own question*) Yup.

*Milton hangs his coat up. Margaret has started laying a trail of newspapers from the front door to the kitchen table. Milton, in his socks, steps cautiously along the newspaper path*

> I felt sure the rain would hold off, so I decided to walk. That's not the first time I've been caught out. I guess you suffer from what they call "a changeable climate" along this coast ...

*Margaret puts a couple of sheets of newspaper down on a chair*

**Margaret**  If you'd park yourself there for now. I've only just this morning done the floor.
**Milton**  I'm pretty dry inside. The coat absorbs the worst of it. I pay a lot of attention to that sort of thing, being out in the elements so much.

*Milton sits, then reaches awkwardly back from his sitting position and with his feet drags some newspaper round so that his feet will be on newspaper while he sits in the chair*

**Margaret**  I'd not long since made some tea. You'll be ready for a cup, Mr ... Farnsworth, did you say? (*She fetches a tray with teapot, cups and milk*)
**Milton**  It might serve to warm me up. Oh, call me Milton, if you would. And you're Margaret, I believe? Though if you'd prefer I call you Mrs —
**Margaret**  Margaret's fine. Oh! (*Sudden panic*) Will you take sugar?
**Milton**  No, no ... Just milk.

*Margaret pours the tea — hands Milton a cup. He's been searching for something to say*

> It's a ... cosy set-up you have here.

**Margaret**  It's small — if that's what you mean.

*Silence*

**Milton** I hope it's OK me calling round like this ...
**Margaret** Well, you're here now, anyway.

*Silence*

**Milton** So you ... work at the store up on the bypass, is that right?
**Margaret** It's not very exciting.
**Milton** Well, I suppose most —
**Margaret** But then job opportunities round here are few and far between.
**Milton** Folk grab what they can, huh? (*Silence*) Have you worked there long?
**Margaret** Five years, now.
**Milton** Ah. (*Silence*) And ... um ... so before that ...?
**Margaret** I was a department manager at the box factory — was there for twenty years. It was a good job, that. They were a nice crowd.
**Milton** So what made you ...?
**Margaret** Damn Yanks came in and bought us out. (*Beat*) Oh, sorry — no offence.
**Milton** None taken.
**Margaret** They closed us down, you see — shifted it abroad.
**Milton** For what it's worth, it's the same in the States right now. I've experienced it myself.
**Margaret** There're kids round here now, Rebecca says, growing up in families where no one in two generations has seen regular work.
**Milton** In a couple of the places I've stayed it seemed everyone was employed in these call centres ...
**Margaret** Trying to sell stuff to those who'd just as soon not know.
**Milton** Not good for the soul, huh?
**Margaret** I wouldn't think so.

*Silence. Less awkward than before*

**Milton** This is very good tea, by the way.
**Margaret** It's nothing fancy. (*Pause*) There's a drop more.

*Milton wasn't really wanting more tea, but she pours some into his cup anyway*

**Milton** So are you serious, Margaret, about me taking a room? Only I bumped into Rebecca last night in Ray's — and she hinted you'd been having second thoughts.

Act I, Scene 3                                                    11

**Margaret**  The whole idea was hers — I'd no chance to object.
**Milton**  I have to say I like her very much. She's sparky. I notice all the fellows treat her with respect.
**Margaret**  She's no one's fool, right enough.
**Milton**  And she gets that from her mother, I presume.

*Margaret is unnerved by this. Milton is aware he's gone too far. After a moment Margaret stands*

**Margaret**  Perhaps you'd like to see the room ...
**Milton**  *(getting up from the table)* Of course —
**Margaret**  But you've not drunk your tea. No, sit down!

*Milton sits*

   I'm sorry, it's a bit awkward, all of this. It'll sound daft, but there's hardly been a man in this house for thirty years, excepting plumbers and so on — who, of course, you tend to know in a place like this.
**Milton**  I understand — it's fine. I'm a bit on edge myself. Rebecca warned me you don't suffer fools.
**Margaret**  That'll be her way of saying I'm rude.

*Margaret busies herself at the sink, washes up her cup, wipes surfaces etc.*

**Milton**  I think she meant you "speak as you find" — is that the phrase? Of course a fellow's always scared he'll be found wanting.
**Margaret**  I'm sure a chap like you wouldn't give a fig what I might think of him.
**Milton**  Listen, Margaret, can I be straight? I'm awkward company; I don't have much in the way of small-talk. What I have got to offer is the promise I can pay and the fact that I'll be out most of the day. I'm not running out of money or anything like that; I'd a budget for this trip and I've got to the point where I feel I'm paying over the odds for substandard fare. Fact is, I'm the kind of man hates to think he's being took for a ride. What more can I say?
**Margaret**  I think we'll rub along fine, Milton — assuming the room's OK. It's small, you'll find, but clean.
**Milton**  Four walls and a bed will do me. And a corner in which to prop my stuff. Oh, there's not much, just a backpack, camera, sketchbooks and whatnot. I've been surrounded by "things" for most my life; it was high time I learned to travel light.
**Margaret**  How long would you need the room for?

**Milton**  I've a week booked in, further South — at the end of the month, before I head home. So ... three weeks at the most.
**Margaret**  We can maybe manage that, without coming to blows. Shall we go up? If you've drunk enough tea?
**Milton**  That'd be great.
**Margaret**  We'll discuss terms if you decide the room suits.

*Margaret moves towards the stairs. Then she realizes Milton hasn't followed. He's unsure if he's permitted to step off from the newspaper.*

**Milton**  Should I ...?
**Margaret**  Your socks look dry enough to me. Though I notice they never were a pair. How must your pictures turn out — if you can't match the colour of your socks?
**Milton**  (*studying his socks*) You got me there.

*Music*

*Black-out*

## Scene 4

*The same. A few days later. Late evening*

*Some light filters through from outside. Otherwise the kitchen is in darkness. There is the sound of the pick-up drawing up outside. Rebecca lets herself in through the back door and turns on the lights. She carries Milton's camera bag and a case of artist's stuff. Milton is close behind carrying his huge back-pack*

*The music fades*

**Milton**  Somehow this doesn't feel right, Rebecca, just barging in ...
**Rebecca**  It's fine. What was the alternative? You lugging this lot up that hill?
**Milton**  I've lugged it all a good way round the coast. I could've managed.
**Rebecca**  She'll not be long, now. I'll wait with you, if you'd like?
**Milton**  I think that might be wise.
**Rebecca**  It never seems to change, this place. There's lino in the bathroom dates back to the Roman occupation.
**Milton**  Well ... if it ain't broke, don't fix it ...
**Rebecca**  If I thought *that* was the reason it wouldn't seem so sad.

Act I, Scene 4                                                          13

**Milton** (*confused*) I'm not sure ...
**Rebecca** Come on, Milton, it's obvious — it's all to do with Dad.
**Milton** I guess people deal with stuff in different ways ...
**Rebecca** It was thirty years ago, for heaven's sake. She could open this place up and charge admission — "How We Used to Live in Days of Yore".
**Milton** If your mother's happy with how things are —
**Rebecca** I'm surprised she hasn't posted up the rules — her "Dos & Don'ts". Of course I imbibed them all with mother's milk; but you're the first stranger to enter her domain. You want a brew?
**Milton** No, I'm good.
**Rebecca** You'll notice, by the way, she unplugs every object not in constant use. I've no idea why. Something she learned from the *Mail*, I guess.
**Milton** The *Mail*?
**Rebecca** The *Daily Mail*. It's a sort of "Danger of Death" manual. "Seventy-five percent of all fatalities are due to domestic appliances. The rest are down to foreign intervention." And if you're not actually *in a* room, all lights must be off. Lids and drawers, that's the other thing. (*She removes the lid from a jar, then pulls a drawer out*) If they're not replaced or closed then the balance of the universe might be disturbed. I couldn't believe she agreed to your staying — it's such a mind-boggling, major lifestyle change.
**Milton** Perhaps you inviting me up here in the first place left her with no option.
**Rebecca** You don't know my mother. No, it's strange but true — she must have really taken a shine to you.
**Milton** I don't feel too comfortable, Rebecca, with this conversation.
**Rebecca** Oh God, Milton, I'm sorry. Should we talk about the weather?
**Milton** Hey, now ...
**Rebecca** Listen, I've beer left in the fridge, you wanna split one?
**Milton** Sure.

*Rebecca retrieves a bottle of beer from the fridge. She gets the bottle opener from the drawer — leaving the drawer open. She pours Milton a glass of beer — she drinks from the bottle*

**Milton** It seems very quiet up here.
**Rebecca** Holiday homes these days mostly, that's why.
**Milton** Does that cause friction?
**Rebecca** No. Oh, there was an incident, a few years ago. Bloke on the end, up from the Midlands. Obsessed with "illegal immigrants" and crime. Built himself one of those hideous metal sheds. Spent his

first summer boasting down at Ray's. Impregnable, he said, keep his precious tools safe — blahdiblah. He goes away one weekend — someone broke into his shed, used his tools to dismantle it, took the shed away, left the tools behind. They were still sat there when he got back. We had a laugh about that. He sold up and left.

**Milton** (*gesturing in the direction of the drive*) I'm guessing you'd need something like a pick-up truck to shift a shed?

**Rebecca** The crime remains unsolved. Cheers.

**Milton** Cheers.

**Rebecca** To your new home. So how goes your painting, by the way?

**Milton** I'm mainly just gathering images, taking photographs and stuff. Ray's been badgering me for a picture, actually.

**Rebecca** He could do with something decent on the walls. Those hunting prints he goes in for have always seemed a bit incongruous.

**Milton** He seems a nice enough fellow. A bit strange — perhaps a bubble short of plumb. He's not local, either, of course ...

**Rebecca** Far from it. He was something in the city, back in the day. Made his pile — then decided he'd like to run a bar by the sea.

**Milton** A "down-sizer", as they say.

**Rebecca** Oh, Ray has bigger plans: a shopping complex a few miles up the road. There are grants for redevelopment, see — plus, land and labour's cheap.

**Milton** A speculator, then?

**Rebecca** Oh, I don't know — these are pretty much ghost towns down this coast — I'm not convinced some crappy mini-mall will bring the punters flooding in.

**Milton** Were you always so cynical?

**Rebecca** (*raising her beer bottle*) It's only my second of the evening. I'll wind down. The more the mellower.

**Milton** Hard day, huh?

**Rebecca** It does get exhausting attempting to make things easier for those poor sods scrabbling about at the bottom of the heap; especially when we're constantly being chopped and changed.

**Milton** But you do still make a difference, all the same?

**Rebecca** Little victories, once in a blue moon, don't always make it seem a life well-spent. So what about you? You ran a business of some sort?

**Milton** Sure. But I'm no saint. Like Ray, I sold up and got out.

**Rebecca** But at one time you employed people — paid wages — created opportunity at least?

**Milton** And won't Ray's mini-mall do that?

**Rebecca** It'll have to be built — that'll mean a few temporary jobs. Then they'll need people to staff the shops. But if you construct a temple to consumerism you need a congregation with spending power or it simply won't sustain. Our local economy was flushed away years ago. That said, to be *seen* to be thinking about doing something scores points.

*The sound of a car drawing up outside*

> Cue much feverish pseudo-activity: feasibility reports, market penetration studies, action plans. In reality, of course, it's the town *centres* that need developing — the *high streets* that need investment. You should be grateful to my mother, Milton, she's saved you from the rest of my tirade.

**Milton**  And just as I was getting interested ...
**Rebecca**  Yeah, right.

*They both laugh*

*Margaret enters with some bags of shopping*

**Margaret**  Were you that eager to move in you couldn't wait for me to get back?
**Rebecca**  I ran into Milton outside Ray's. Saw how he was struggling with his stuff. I sent you a text, though I said you'd be unlikely to have your phone with you.

*Margaret shuts the open drawer and replaces the lid on the jar*

**Milton**  Margaret, I hope we haven't —
**Margaret**  There's no harm done, Milton. I could've picked you up myself if you'd said.

*Margaret turns on the table lamp, then starts unpacking and putting away the shopping. Rebecca helps*

**Milton**  Pete kindly let us use his truck. He seemed happy to remain at Ray's.
**Margaret**  Why he drives that ugly great thing I've never known. It's not as if he's done a day's work in his life — of the labouring kind.
**Rebecca**  Pete inherited the pick-up from his brother, as Mother knows. And it's perfectly all right for running round.
**Margaret**  Pete's brother, of course, knew what work was.
**Rebecca**  Pete's brother was a builder. He went bankrupt. (*Taking some items from one of the shopping bags*) Looks like you've been piling on the loyalty points.

**Margaret**  I felt inspired to try out a few new dishes. Milton, I hope you're not a vegetarian. (*She places a bottle of wine on the table*)
**Milton**  I'll eat most anything that's put before me.
**Margaret**  Rebecca, did you think to make my guest a cup of tea?
**Rebecca**  We're on the beer. I thought it needed using up.
**Margaret**  It would save me keep moving it round whenever I go to the fridge. Now, Milton, have you eaten?
**Milton**  I grabbed a burger from the van down at the harbour.
**Margaret**  Then you've risked a lethal dose of salmonella. The least we can do is improve your eating habits. You can't go through life on greasy takeaways.
**Rebecca**  I should get back on down to Ray's. Keep Pete company.
**Milton**  Hey, Margaret, why don't we head down there and join them? Have a drink to mark my moving in? We could stroll back in the moonlight — the night air would do us good — what d'you say?

*Rebecca has been shaking her head behind Margaret's back*

**Margaret**  I don't think so, Milton. I'm happy to be home; I'm just gonna put my feet up and relax. But you must come and go as you choose.
**Milton**  Perhaps I'd best have an early night, Rebecca — get settled in. Besides, I've my journal to write.
**Rebecca**  Your what?
**Milton**  It was actually Pete's idea. I've been persuaded — very much against my will — to talk to my local arts club about this trip. Pete suggested I start keeping a journal, base my presentation on that.
**Margaret**  You go off and have your drink, Milton. You can take the spare front door key. It's on the hook, Rebecca.
**Milton**  Well if you're sure ... But I really ought to get this junk out of your way ...
**Margaret**  I'll take it up presently, leave it where it is.
**Milton**  No, I insist, it's *my* responsibility; it'll be sorted out the minute I get back.
**Margaret**  I suppose it won't hurt where it is for now.
**Rebecca**  Milt? (*She throws the key to him*) I'll pop by soon, Mum. (*As she leaves*) You fit then, Milton?

*Rebecca leaves*

**Milton**  Guess I'm as fit as I'll ever be, eh Margaret? (*Pause*) Given my diet of dubious meat and grease ...
**Margaret**  If you hang about here much longer, Milton, you'll run into yourself coming back.

Act I, Scene 5                                                                 17

**Milton**  Got that. I'll see you at breakfast.
**Margaret**  I dare say.

*Hesitantly, Milton leaves*

*The sound of the pick-up starting up and driving away*

*Margaret goes to the window and watches them drive away. She thinks, then turns the outside light on. She removes the bottle of wine from the table and puts it away. She turns the upstairs light on and then goes to turn the table lamp off. She is about to go up when she notices Milton's stuff. With some effort she picks it up*

*She turns off the main light and struggles off upstairs*

*Music*

*Black-out*

## Scene 5

*The same. Early the next morning*

*Milton, in his robe and espadrilles in the yard, has been watching the sunrise*

*The music fades*

**Milton**  There are days when sunrise can still seem a miracle of sorts. Bowden Broome would rise at four and be out on the shore to watch the first rays stripe the water. He'd make rough watercolour sketches — and along the edges of these sketches he'd write notes in his tiny, spidery hand — describing the colours and effects. A few years ago, when Sotheby's in London auctioned a book of these sketches, a telephone bidder paid the equivalent of a hundred thousand dollars for the privilege of owning these scrawls and reflections. What would Bowden Broome have made of that? He'd been careful with money all his life. He was a scruffy man by all accounts, clothes interested him as little as did things. After his death a reporter from the Augusta Chronicle was sent to write a piece about his house. She commented that she found it almost impossible to believe so much beauty could emerge from such squalor. And yet — there were women. Three unhappy wives. In the sketches that he made of the first she glowers out at us as if musing on a curse. I've never painted people. My wife once remarked that I should; that way, she suggested, I could at least make someone happy through my art. But to look upon one's likeness is a dubious pleasure, I believe. To view oneself as seen through other eyes? That way, surely — only disappointment lies.

*The Lights come up on the kitchen. Margaret has put some bread in the toaster and is cooking scrambled eggs. Milton comes through and stands in the doorway unobserved. After a few seconds he speaks*

**Milton** Good morning, Margaret.
**Margaret** Oh, good Lord, you startled me. I'd ... I thought I'd do eggs — scrambled, if that's all right ...?

*Margaret is avoiding looking at Milton*

**Milton** Scrambled eggs sounds perfect. (*Pause*) I watched the sun rise. Never ceases to fill me with wonder.
**Margaret** I always put pepper in. And milk. I don't know why. Some don't. But I do. My mother did them that way too.
**Milton** Margaret, have I offended you?
**Margaret** You've not been stood there more than a minute, so I don't see how you could've.
**Milton** You just seem — for some reason — singularly unable to look at me today.
**Margaret** It's unusual that's all. A half-naked, fully-grown man stood standing in my kitchen.

*Milton opens his robe to reveal a tatty old t-shirt and boxer shorts*

**Milton** Is this what concerns you? Margaret?

*She looks, then quickly looks away*

I'm quite decent. There's little danger of anything untoward popping out.
**Margaret** (*quickly*) And did you have a pleasant evening at Ray's?
**Milton** Oh, sure. He's an interesting fellah — Rebecca's Pete, I mean. And soon to be a published poet. (*Pause*) Of course, I take on board that you've no time for him.
**Margaret** She could do better's all I think.
**Milton** They seem to be very much in love. Isn't that enough?
**Margaret** You'll have toast I suppose?

## Act I, Scene 5

**Milton**  I won't mention Pete again, if that's what you'd prefer. And in future I'll ensure I'm fully dressed before I make my entrance.
**Margaret**  You must do exactly as you'd do at home.
**Milton**  At home I wander round as naked as a babe. (*He sits at the table*)
**Margaret**  (*swiftly changing the subject*) Will one piece of toast be enough?
**Milton**  Just as it comes.

*Margaret puts the food on the table, then hovers, waiting for Milton to commence eating. Milton eats through what follows. First he pushes the egg off the toast — then he eats the egg with his fork — then he picks up and eats the toast*

**Margaret**  I'm not used to change. Rebecca thinks it ridiculous, but I get nervous if I have to go somewhere strange. Or talk to people I don't know. I'm not like her or you, I'm not ...
**Milton**  What?
**Margaret**  I can't always *think* what to say.
**Milton**  OK ...
**Margaret**  Like when Pete showed me one of his poems — then asked me what I thought. I felt ... I don't know ... foolish.
**Milton**  What was the poem about?
**Margaret**  I think it was about how there used to be more singing — in communities — how people used to meet to sing together — and now they don't so much. And how it's a shame things turned out that way.
**Milton**  And what did you think about that?
**Margaret**  Well ... I thought ... it was true.
**Milton**  So why didn't you say so?
**Margaret**  It would've sounded odd.
**Milton**  Maybe, to you. But if a fellow's a poet of any sort — to have someone say they found their poem "true" — should be high praise indeed.
**Margaret**  I didn't know.
**Milton**  Listen, Margaret — you do OK. You've raised a child alone, you hold down a job ...
**Margaret**  Oh, I'm fine at work because I know exactly what I have to do. That's different.
**Milton**  You're nobody's fool, Margaret, trust me. But if you feel so ... exposed ... can I ask you why on earth you took me in?
**Margaret**  I suppose I thought I ought to make an effort — to not be so ... predictable. Plus, I got intrigued. You seemed so ... relaxed. I know *you* don't think so.
**Milton**  A little too relaxed — it turns out.

**Margaret**  A breath of fresh air, I suppose I thought you'd be.
**Milton**  And in the cold light of day? Now you've seen me in my rough and rugged, crumpled morning state?
**Margaret**  You do look funny, it's true.
**Milton**  Well, they do say, don't they, if you can make a woman laugh you're halfway there. (*Embarrassed*) Not that I ...
**Margaret**  When I was a child we lived in the last house in the row. Our backyard faced on to the moors. We'd get tramps turn up for food. Men who'd come over the hills, down to our back door. And Mother would always make them a sandwich and a drink. She had the attitude "there but for the grace of God ..." you know? I was always quite excited when one of these poor souls arrived. They'd sit eating in the yard and I'd stare — wondering where they'd come from and why. Imagining what *their* world was like. The terrible freedom of always moving on. My life seemed so well mapped out — I'd meet a man and marry him and that would be that.
**Milton**  Wait a minute — (*he opens his robe*) — Are you saying I'm like some old bum who's turned up at your door?
**Margaret**  Stop it. You *do* make me laugh. (*She busies herself again*) It's not healthy harking back, I suppose. But there are times when all you do is think about the past.
**Milton**  That's very wise ...
**Margaret**  Is it?
**Milton**  It sure rings a bunch of bells with me. Hey Margaret, what say you come on out with me today? The company would make a pleasant change.
**Margaret**  I've got to work.
**Milton**  Well you must get *some* time off. When's your next free day?
**Margaret**  Monday, I suppose. It depends on the other girls. I'm the one always has to cover.
**Milton**  Well, Margaret, why not make a change? On Monday you and I will hit the road. We could load up your jalopy and just go. Take a picnic, find a bay. What d'you say?
**Margaret**  I don't know ...
**Milton**  Then that's settled — it's a date! (*Quickly*) I don't mean "date" date, Margaret, I just mean — "a date in my diary" kinda date. (*Swiftly changing the subject*) But hey, these eggs, Margaret, I gotta say, are quite superb.

*Margaret looks at him and smiles*

*Music*

*Black-out*

## Scene 6

*The coastal path. A few days later*

*The sound of seabirds. Margaret looks out to sea. Milton takes photographs. They are some way apart to begin with*

*Music fades*

**Margaret**  It's been so long since I stood up here, you wouldn't believe. I'd bring Rebecca out for walks sometimes, with a couple of the other wives. The kids would go haring off — used to frighten the life out of me. (*Pause*) Sometimes Rebecca would spot a trawler and come running up — want to know if it was Daddy coming back. (*Pause*) You never forget ...
**Milton**  Forget what?
**Margaret**  That *life* — the way things were. (*She smiles*) All those strange superstitions — things we dare not do.
**Milton**  Like what?
**Margaret**  Like when a man packed his bag before he left; once something had been packed it couldn't be taken out, that would bring bad luck. And we never waved them off from the house. If we had, then they thought once they were at sea, a wave might come and wash them off the deck. Oh ... and then after they'd left, things like ashtrays and teapots couldn't be emptied 'til at least the next day — so it didn't seem we were wishing them away. Some wives wouldn't empty ashtrays again 'til their men got back. I thought that a bit extreme. Then there were the things they thought they mustn't see — on their way to the boats.
**Milton**  What sort of things?
**Margaret**  Well, a clergyman, that meant bad luck. Some men, if they saw one, would turn back, refuse to go. And you'd always to make sure your man had emptied his pockets of change before he left. 'Cos if not he'd just throw it all to the kids down at the dock. And if there were no kids about — they'd just chuck all their coins in the sea. Daft, really.
**Milton**  Risk breeds superstition, I guess.
**Margaret**  Yes. And you'd to go along with it, as the men needed to feel safe. Though it made not a jot of difference. There's no riskier way to make a living.

*A jet-fighter flies over, very low. Milton ducks*

**Milton**  Jeez! They scare the shit out of me! Sorry.

**Margaret**  When Rebecca was little she'd get scared. She thought that if we left the landing light on a plane might crash into the house. *Landing* light?
**Milton**  (*unconvincingly*) I got that. Is it true that many of the fishermen refused to learn to swim?
**Margaret**  They preferred it that way. They thought, if they were swept overboard, to resist would just prolong the struggle. Though it's difficult to imagine them going down without a fight. They were strong men. Fit men.
**Milton**  But no man is stronger than the sea?
**Margaret**  Later on, Rebecca made up a game. She called it "All the things that Daddy could not say". There were certain words, you see, they'd never use while on the boat. She made a little pack of cards — wrote one word on each — with a drawing. I remember she insisted they'd to be kept in a certain order. She made me memorize it so I'd get it right when I tidied up her toys.
**Milton**  Had any of the fishermen ever heard of Bowden Broome?
**Margaret**  My husband was a *trawlerman*, Milton. Fishermen — he'd say — stand safely on riverbanks with rods. That's a hobby. A trawlerman was a different breed. Oh yes, we'd all heard of Bowden Broome. They'd speak of him in school. And occasionally there'd be articles in the local news. But I think now, to younger folk, it just seems so long ago. "Ancient history" ...
**Milton**  (*disappointed*) Sure. (*Pause*) You're not cold?
**Margaret**  I'm fine. Though I don't understand you and your camera. I thought you were a painter. Isn't taking a picture cheating?
**Milton**  It's easier this way. I can then work on the paintings somewhere nice and warm. If Bowden Broome had owned a digital camera he might have enjoyed better health.
**Margaret**  Tell me if I'm standing in your way.
**Milton**  You needn't worry, I seldom photograph people. They don't interest me. To photograph, I mean. To paint.
**Margaret**  I used to like taking pictures of Rebecca. It's nice to have a record of them growing up. Though it was a devil of a job just getting her to stop still long enough. If you never had kids you wouldn't know —
**Milton**  Oh, I did.
**Margaret**  Really? I just assumed —
**Milton**  A son. Frank. He died. Fifteen years ago. (*He starts packing up*) We should head back down to the bay, clear up our picnic. I'm desperate for a drink, all of a sudden. We should have brought along some beer — or perhaps wine.

Act I, Scene 7                                                                23

**Margaret**  That's my fault. I didn't think. There's wine at home. And there's Rebecca's beer, still cluttering up the fridge.
**Milton**  It would certainly help round off the day.
**Margaret**  I'm really sorry, Milton, about your son.
**Milton**  We'd best not hang about. It looks like rain.

*Black-out*

*Music*

## Scene 7

*Margaret's kitchen. The evening of the same day*

*On the table the remains of a meal and an empty wine bottle. Margaret is preparing a cafetière of coffee*

*Music fades*

*Milton mops up what's left on his plate with some bread*

**Milton**  There's nothing quite so good as home-made bolognese. (*In a cod-Italian accent*) "Spaghetti lika mamma useta make"!

*Margaret realizes the wine bottle is empty. She fetches a fresh one from the fridge and hands it to Milton to open*

**Margaret**  D'you know, Milton, I don't think I've ever opened two bottles of wine on the same night.
**Milton**  (*opening the wine*) Fear not, Margaret. For 'tis I have consumed the lion's share. (*He studies the bottle before pouring wine into their glasses*) Who would have believed happiness could come so cheap?
**Margaret**  I can't remember when I last had a proper drink ... it must be — (*she remembers*) — one of the girls at work asked me to her wedding. We should be ashamed of ourselves, don't you think?
**Milton**  *Au contraire*, I too haven't had this much fun since ... God knows. Since God was a boy, I suppose. But it does you good now and again, don't you think, to ... (*in an English accent*) "get blotto". To proclaim ... "Bottoms up"!

*They drink*

And "down the hatch".

**Margaret** I'm sure I'll suffer for this ...
**Milton** The trick is not to think about it. *Regrette rien. (With difficulty) Non, je ne regrette rien.*
**Margaret** That's easy for you to say.
**Milton** Actually, it's not.
**Margaret** That's what I meant.
**Milton** *Touché.* My poor brain is shutting down. (*As Stan Laurel*) You must wake me up in case I go to sleep.
**Margaret** You're not making sense, Milton.
**Milton** (*as Stan Laurel*) Indeed I don't. Ah well, the coffee will help us get our second wind. The night is young, goddammit! (*Pause*) And we are old.
**Margaret** Not so much of the "we".
**Milton** OK, just me. But you know what, Margaret?

*He sings, badly, the first two lines of the song Sinatra sang so beautifully — "You Make Me Feel So Young". He then realizes that he can't remember how the song continues*

Um ... "dum-di-di-doo ... dee-di-di-dum ..." And so on. Oh, I can definitely carry a tune, Margaret, don't you agree?
**Margaret** Well, it depends how high you set your standards.

*There's the sound of a car drawing up outside*

Oh dear, who's that? Don't say my wayward darling daughter has returned.
**Milton** Mum's the word.
**Margaret** We'll pretend nothing untoward has happened.
**Milton** Nothing has.
**Margaret** I mean, pretend we're not ... pretend we're just ...
**Milton** Pretend that we're not really having fun?
**Margaret** That's the one.
**Milton** (*feigning extreme drunkenness*) I will be the very shoul of dishcretion.
**Margaret** Stop it, Milton — act sober.

*Rebecca enters*

**Rebecca** Evening all.
**Milton** (*deliberately*) I swear to you, Rebecca, we weren't doing anything even a little untoward.
**Margaret** Milton!

Act I, Scene 7                                                    25

**Rebecca**  What's going on?
**Margaret**  I confess, Rebecca, I am a little drunk.
**Milton**  Wait a minute, I thought we'd agreed —
**Margaret**  It just slipped out.
**Milton**  I admit that we both have taken drink. But in our defence — we're both responsible adults.
**Margaret**  And I have humbly made coffee, too.
**Rebecca**  Hey ... if you kids're having fun, what's the problem?
**Milton**  Oh, no. Don't get the wrong idea. We're definitely not having fun. Nothing could be further from our minds.
**Margaret**  We simply set out to put the world to rights.
**Milton**  And then got distracted somewhere down the road. So I suggested we drink some more. To help us remember ... what was it?
**Margaret**  Where we were ...
**Milton**  ... Before we got waylaid.
**Rebecca**  Well that sounds sensible enough. I'll join you if I may.

*She pours herself a glass of wine. It doesn't taste good*

**Margaret**  You wouldn't prefer a cup of coffee?
**Rebecca**  I don't anymore, I told you. My headaches?
**Milton**  Very wise. Stick with wine.
**Margaret**  No one's *ever* suffered ill effects from wine.
**Rebecca**  So I was just nipping to Ray's for a beer. Figured Milton might need rescuing. I'm kidding. Thought he might fancy a change of scenery. Pete mentioned you hadn't been in for a few days. Even *Chez* Ray himself remarked on your absence, don't you know.
**Margaret**  Well, Milton, you *are* a popular chap.
**Milton**  I'm ashamed to say it's true, Rebecca, my attendance rate is shoddy. But I fear that won't be remedied tonight.
**Margaret**  We've been out and about, for the best part of the day.
**Milton**  I asked your mother to accompany me on one of my trips. And much to my surprise — and great pleasure, indeed — she agreed.
**Margaret**  We took along a picnic, but I neglected to pack any booze.
**Milton**  So this is lunch and dinner's consignment, rolled into one.
**Rebecca**  Well, just so long as you're aware of how she gets.
**Margaret**  And how do I get, exactly?
**Rebecca**  Sick ... usually.
**Margaret**  I resemble that remark.
**Rebecca**  I refer you to Iko Taylor's wedding reception.
**Margaret**  That was a different matter altogether. That was food poisoning.
**Rebecca**  It was a set menu — and you were the only one got sick.

**Milton**  Your mother, Rebecca, is safe enough with me. I've cleaned up plenty of vomit in my time — and not just my own.
**Margaret**  What is all this? I'm not going to be sick.
**Rebecca**  Just so long as you know what you're letting yourself in for, Milton. There's a mop and bucket out back and bleach under the sink. In the morning you'll notice little veins have popped out under her eyes and her nose has gone pink. But for heaven's sake don't point this out, 'cos it'll make her cry — and once she turns on the taps, she never stops. And you've to keep your distance and stay silent for at least twelve hours — during which the only words she'll utter are "Never ... again". So ... having fully briefed you, I believe my work here is done. (*She downs her drink and grimaces*) Behave yourselves.
**Milton**  I shall endeavour to call in at the bar — perhaps tomorrow, Rebecca.
**Rebecca**  Whenever. Bye.

*Rebecca leaves*

**Milton**  Oh, remember me to Pete ... and to Ray.

*The sound of a car driving off. Left once again alone, the pair seem more sober. The atmosphere has changed*

**Margaret**  Strange how sometimes your offspring can make you feel *you're* the child.
**Milton**  She cares, is all. It's kinda sweet how she feels she oughta look out for her ma.
**Margaret**  (*pouring herself more wine*) May as well be hung for a sheep as a lamb.
**Milton**  (*pouring himself another glass*) And I've my reputation to consider — my absence having been noted at (*in an English accent*) "the local hostelry". (*He raises his glass to clink with Margaret's*) To Rebecca. Cheers.
**Margaret**  Cheers.
**Milton**  She's a terrific young woman. You're very lucky, Margaret, believe me.
**Margaret**  It wasn't always easy.
**Milton**  You have every reason be proud. She's healthy, she's happy — and she's here.
**Margaret**  And I should be more accepting of Pete?
**Milton**  It's not my place to interfere.

*Silence*

## Act I, Scene 7

**Margaret**  What happened to your son? I mean, if you don't want to ——
**Milton**  It's fine. (*Pause*) He'd just turned twenty-three. His mother had always hoped he'd join the family business — but he went his own way. Joined the Marines. I didn't approve, I guess — but I kept my mouth shut — it was what *he* wanted to do. They were on a training exercise down in South Carolina. He'd just before been home on leave. His mother had thrown him a birthday bash — proud friends and neighbours, that kind of thing. Though it was more for her benefit, I think. She always got a kick out of showing Frank off. Her big brave boy. (*Pause*) A few days later we got the call. They said he'd drowned — which seemed to make no sense. He'd got certificates for swimming all through school. But they carry all this kit on exercise — and from what they said — he just went under and ... never came back up.
**Margaret**  I'm sorry, Milton.
**Milton**  I can't even pretend we were close. That's the worst of it. It wasn't until he was gone I started to wonder ... who he was. Oh, I knew the basics. He was a competitive boy — ambitious — to get on in the Marines. He was his mother's son — not a bit like me.
**Margaret**  Oh, I'm sure every lad ——
**Milton**  No. I wish he had taken after me. 'Cos if he'd been feckless and slovenly he'd still be here. Stinking up the room over the garage, borrowing my car and bringing it home with the tank empty and the ashtray full. Doing all the things a son's supposed to do. Disliking and disrespecting me — I wouldn't mind. You know what it is I never stop regretting? I wish I'd hugged him once or twice and slapped his back; wish I'd shown I understood what his achievements meant to him. That's why when it comes to Rebecca you've gotta be glad. She's pretty much sorted. And that fellow of hers, he's sound. He won't ever be rich — but he writes his stuff — and he makes her proud. And when you see them together, it's touching — how "at one" they seem, how happy *in-the-moment* ... you know? Shoot, I'm sorry, I get that I just did exactly what I said I wouldn't do.
**Margaret**  It would have been different had her father been about. (*Pause*) Every time the boats went out, we knew they might not come back. You learn to live with that. But you're never properly prepared. How can you be? All the time you wait in dread, for that knock. (*Pause*) We used to fight like cat and dog, her father and me. Over money mostly. They did all right, but then they'd get back to shore — and have to drink. "Three Day Millionaires" they used to call them. His father had been a trawlerman too. It was all he really knew, and men who risk their lives at work grow close. I used to think — you've just spent three weeks with these men, why must you now go drinking

with them? But you put up with it, 'cos that's how life was. There wasn't much romance, to be honest. Of course that didn't mean ... When he was taken it was still a kick in the teeth. But I'd Rebecca to bring up, so I'd to just carry on. (*Pause*) I sometimes think it's best he went the way he did. Doing what he loved. There was still an industry then. He was proud, he cared about his trade. I don't know what he'd have made of life here now.

**Milton** He'd still have you. And Rebecca.

**Margaret** Don't get me wrong, what we had *worked* — in a way. Three weeks gone, seventy-two hours home. (*Pause*) He could be kind. Once he'd wound down from where he'd been. When he laid off the drink. There'd be a day or two perhaps when we were man and wife. Who knows how we'd have coped with normal life? He was never easy-going. We were probably too much alike.

**Milton** Margaret, you're all right.

**Margaret** Bitter and twisted, is what I am.

**Milton** I wouldn't say that.

*Silence*

**Margaret** So you and your wife ...?

**Milton** She walked out — 'bout a year after Frank died. Oh, I understood. Everything — to her — came to seem ... meaningless. (*Pause*) We just ... couldn't make it work.

**Margaret** I'm sure you did your best, Milton.

**Milton** Well, we go on. Try to make the most of what's left. Though things can't be the same, it's still a life. We all have regrets, we've all made mistakes. We all act dumb and learn too late. Am I right?

**Margaret** Yes.

**Milton** But you put it behind you — hope to fare better next time. Here, now — this moment — life's OK.

*Silence. Margaret drinks. She realizes she's had enough*

**Margaret** I should turn in. (*She gets up — wobbles, steadies herself on the table*) Oh, I think I might be drunk.

**Milton** And tired, no doubt — of Milt's old-timey, Hallmark wisdom.

**Margaret** I think you're very kind and thoughtful.

**Milton** I'm an old fart — who's talked too much.

**Margaret** No. I've enjoyed tonight. But I really should clear up.

**Milton** (*getting up*) And I really should assist.

**Margaret** No. Sod it — it'll keep 'til tomorrow.

Act I, Scene 7                                                        29

*They're close. Margaret kisses Milton on the cheek, clumsily. He's surprised. So is she*

**Margaret**  I don't know why I did that.

*She tries to embrace and kiss him more passionately. He backs off — but she holds on*

**Milton**  Margaret, stop.
**Margaret**  I'm taking your advice. Living for the moment, like you said.
**Milton**  (*trying to remove himself from her embrace*) Come on, let's get you to bed.
**Margaret**  God, Milton, I thought you'd never ask.
**Milton**  That isn't what I meant. (*Loudly, with authority*) Margaret!

*His tone gets through. Margaret backs off and moves away from him. Milton also moves away from her and momentarily faces away from her*

**Margaret**  I'm sorry, Milton — I must be a bit confused.
**Milton**  Well hey, Margaret — welcome to the club.

*Milton looks at Margaret — sees she's about to cry — softens — attempts to reassure her*

  Oh, now ... Everything's *fine*, Margaret. Everything's just fine.

*Black-out*

## ACT II

### Scene 1

*The yard. The next morning*

*Music. Milton is out in the yard, fully dressed. He is just finishing eating some sweets. He screws a wrapper up and puts it in his pocket*

*Music fades*

**Milton**  What you see may not be exactly what it seems. One of Bowden Broome's largest works in oils — *The Empty Coracle* — painted in the winter of nineteen-o-eight — shows a sea becalmed; in the distance bobs the vessel that gives the work its name. There's a school of thought believes there's more to this piece than meets the eye. A faint, pale line on the furthest edge of the boat has been claimed to represent a human presence — the knuckles of a man about to climb aboard, a grasping hand crawling up the side. I'm not convinced. I believe that scrawly line is simply ... light. *The* Empty *Coracle*. What does that title say? If the preceding narrative of the painting is of a storm-tossed boat, then we can safely assume its occupant has drowned.

*Milton enters the house*

> *As he does so Margaret emerges down the stairs. She's a bit the worse for wear. She pours a glass of water — finds some pills etc.*

**Milton**  Well, good-morning, Margaret.
**Margaret**  Never again.
**Milton**  I'm betting it was something you ate ...
**Margaret**  I think it's best if no one speaks.
**Milton**  I thought I'd grab breakfast out.
**Margaret**  That's probably wise.
**Milton**  Just wanted to check you were all right.
**Margaret**  I'll be fine. It'll just take time. Thank goodness I'm not at work 'til one.
**Milton**  I'll catch you later on then. If you're *sure* that you're all right?
**Margaret**  *Please*, Milton — just *go*.

Act II, Scene 2

**Milton** I'm gone. (*He picks up his stuff, heads for the door*) Oh ... I was thinking we might ask Rebecca for a meal. I'd like to cook. I do a mean lasagne ... if that's OK with you?
**Margaret** Oh God, Milton.
**Milton** You don't care for lasagne?
**Margaret** I can't think about it now.
**Milton** I'll sort it out. How does Thursday week sound? You're on earlies, most Thursdays, am I right?

*No reply*

Thursday week it is then. I'll see you later. (*He heads for the door. At the last minute he stops*) Oh ... (*He gets a bottle of apple juice out of the fridge, places it before her*) Drink that, it'll help.

*He goes*

*Margaret suddenly remembers what happened last night. She puts her head in her hands*

*Music*

*Black-out*

### Scene 2

*The coastal path. A week later*

*The sound of seabirds. Milton is out with his camera and his sketch book. The camera is on a tripod*

*Music fades*

*Milton looks through the viewfinder of his camera. Rebecca appears in his line of sight*

**Rebecca** You never stop, it seems.
**Milton** Time's running out. I need to capture it all before I leave.
**Rebecca** I saw the car down on the road. I thought Mum would be with you.
**Milton** She loaned it me to get supplies. It's not strictly legal, I know, but there you go.

**Rebecca**  She has been behaving pretty strangely of late.
**Milton**  Is that so?

*A jet-fighter hurtles by overhead. Milton ducks*

**Milton**  Shit!
**Rebecca**  You don't need to duck, Milton — they're at least three hundred feet up.
**Milton**  That's reassuring.
**Rebecca**  They *are* going about seven miles per minute, of course. So the margin for error is slight.
**Milton**  Right.
**Rebecca**  Tonkas and Tiffies from Lossie.
**Milton**  We are, indeed, divided by a common language.
**Rebecca**  Tornados and Typhoons from Lossiemouth. It's mostly only during the day. At night you get the bigger traffic — heading out over the Atlantic. (*Pause*) Don't you ever get bored of the sea?
**Milton**  I was brought up in a small desert town, 'bout as far from the sea as you can get. Never set eyes on the ocean 'til I was twenty-one.
**Rebecca**  We take it for granted, I suppose.
**Milton**  Never forget that first time we drove to the coast. Me and a coupla friends from home. The excitement when we saw for the first time that glimmer of light on water. Stopped the car right there and got out — just to freeze that moment in our minds. Those were two happy weeks living on the beach. The other guys chased girls and lived it up — I mostly stared out at the waves. That was it for me. I've kept her close ever since. I can see the Atlantic from my home. (*Pause*) Are you still on for supper Thursday?
**Rebecca**  Sure. (*Pause*) I popped in to see Mum yesterday.
**Milton**  She said.
**Rebecca**  It's funny ... you know ... seeing how she's changed.
**Milton**  Her *life* has changed. With you leaving home, I mean.
**Rebecca**  It's not just that.

*Milton turns his attention to his camera*

**Milton**  So how's Pete?
**Rebecca**  He's great. They may be putting one of his poems up on a train. It's one of these "culture meets commerce" projects. The plan is to commission local artists and writers to make work which celebrates the region.
**Milton**  Great ...
**Rebecca**  But you know Pete, his first idea was about how the sea was over-fished, and how there's no industry along this coast these days

## Act II, Scene 2

— blahdiblah. I told him that's not what they'd want. So he got all stroppy thinking he'd have to compromise. But, like I said, all through history artists have had to be careful not to bite the hand that feeds. You know this stuff, I guess ...

**Milton** Sure. Some of Bowden Broome's least impressive works were the commissions he struggled to fulfil. Portraits painted in the gardens of the wealthy. Politician's pets. Pampered wives. He resented those jobs so much he'd sometimes neglect to sign his name.

**Rebecca** Like I said to Pete, you've to pitch it right. Once you've sold the concept you're free to ... exercise a little ambiguity. So then he got into it again. He's come up with three ideas.

**Milton** I'd like to hear them sometime.

**Rebecca** I'll tell him. Or you can. If you're popping into Ray's.

**Milton** I'd thought I'd maybe drop by tonight.

**Rebecca** It's really odd — once he's fired up, it's difficult to even drag him to the pub. But he likes talking to you. You seem to sort of understand what he does. He'll be sorry to see you go.

**Milton** I've over a week left yet.

**Rebecca** I should be off — I've a departmental meeting at one. Oh ... by the way ... you and Mum ... are you, like, sleeping together?

**Milton** Even if we were, Rebecca, would that be any of your business?

**Rebecca** I just don't want to see her get hurt.

**Milton** Me neither.

*Silence*

**Rebecca** I really should go.
**Milton** Right.
**Rebecca** Listen, Milt ... no offence meant, yeah?
**Milton** None taken, I guess.
**Rebecca** (*touching him on the arm*) Friends?
**Milton** Sure.
**Rebecca** Later, then.

*Rebecca leaves*

**Milton** (*to himself*) Later.

*Milton runs both hands back through his hair. He puffs out his cheeks. He takes sweets from his pocket and starts to eat*

*Music*

*Black-out*

## Scene 3

*Margaret's kitchen. A few days later. Night*

*There is debris on the table from the meal. Milton and Margaret are sitting at the table. Rebecca fetches a beer from the fridge*

*Music fades*

**Rebecca** That's it. Last one. The sole remaining trace of me. Should I leave it ... as a monument, perhaps?
**Margaret** Just drink it — and leave me with a nice, well-ordered fridge.
**Rebecca** It's good to have ambitions, I suppose.
**Margaret** For all you know, Rebecca, I may have hidden depths.
**Milton** (*changing the subject*) So what's the verdict then, on Milt's famous "Lasagne Lika Mama Useta Make"?
**Margaret** It was very nice, Milton.
**Rebecca** And well worth the wait.
**Milton** My wife used to say: "Milt's willing ... but he works at his own pace".

*Margaret takes plates to the sink*

**Margaret** He bought a brand new chopping knife, you know. My cutlery's not good enough for him.
**Rebecca** Your cutlery belongs in a museum. (*Pause*) So Milton, we've established you can cook. The next question has to be: and are you rich?
**Margaret** Rebecca!

*Milton gets up, goes to the fridge, pours himself some apple juice*

**Milton** Well now, you may not believe it, Rebecca — but the fact is, I am. A caring capitalist, I like to think. And an accidental one, at that.
**Rebecca** You mean you inherited your wealth?
**Milton** Not at all. Made it all ourselves — my wife and me. What I meant was: I didn't try. Not to blow my own trumpet, but I'm also a brand name and a marketing resource.
**Rebecca** Now I really *am* intrigued. So come on, Milton, spill the beans, we're on the edge of our seats.
**Margaret** *You* may be, dear, not me.

Act II, Scene 3                                                      35

**Rebecca**  You've gotta be a little bit interested, at least. We could be in the presence of a bona fide, rich celebrity here. Go ahead, Milt, you have the floor.

*Margaret sits back at the table. Milton paces*

**Milton**  OK. So it all began quite small. Very small, in fact. With bees.
**Rebecca**  By "bees" you mean the little buzzy things?
**Milton**  Beautiful and busy honey bees.
**Rebecca**  Go on ...
**Milton**  I was thirty years old. I'd settled in Maine. Despite my parents' hopes, I'd refused to get a trade. But I could do odd-jobs just fine, so, for the most part, that's what I did. I'd no projected "career arc", no dreams of "getting on". I'd happily spend the whole day making sketches if there were no other calls on my time. I'd rented a tumbledown house, with some land — and bought some bees. And I was happy as a hog in muck just doing as I pleased. I'd make honey and sell it from the roadside. It came in peanut-butter jars with poorly-printed labels on the side. "Milt's Honey" — no whizzo marketing for me. That's until I met my wife — who one fine day pulled in to try my wares. That was "day one" of my empire you might say — 'cos boy, did she turn out to be a gal with a plan. Those little jars were just the start. Next came beeswax candles — hand-dipped of course. Then lip balm, perfumed body oil, polishes, crayons, pet-care products ... I could go on. But it was the personal grooming stuff made the bucks. And the trick we used was to always *seem* small. That great marketing myth — the family firm. I was the face on the jar: a backwoods, bearded good-ol' boy — stood there like some hick beside his hive — Milt Farnsworth and his gosh-darn bees. Corny – but it worked. In next to no time we grew from hawking the stuff at regional craft fairs to a turn-over of one hundred and twenty million bucks a year. Those products are now used by movie actors, sport stars, news anchors, supermodels — even president's wives. And so it goes. When the marriage went south we sold up and got out. But I remain the face — and the name. The company pay me a retainer every year to turn up at launches, functions and so on — where I stand around looking scruffy and confused — scratching my beard. For some reason folk find that quaint. And there you have the story of my corporate life. It all began with bees. And none of it had much to do with me. (*He sits back at the table*)
**Rebecca**  Wow.
**Margaret**  Wow, indeed.
**Rebecca**  But wait a minute, if you're so rich, how come you're so mean?

**Margaret** Rebecca!
**Milton** "Mean"?
**Rebecca** Tight. You know ... *careful*? This isn't exactly the Hilton, right?
**Milton** Oh, I see. Well, after the business was sold, I splurged a bit, I guess. Then after a few years I started to take stock. And I realized – OK, I have a house, some land and what passes for my health; I didn't see the need for much else. So I set up a Foundation. To help sufferers from Post Traumatic Stress Disorder. In memory of my son. He ... uh, he died, Rebecca ...
**Rebecca** That's rough. I'm sorry.
**Milton** Sure.
**Rebecca** Well — and you said you weren't a saint ...
**Milton** Oh, now. I don't talk about this stuff generally. Now I feel kinda —
**Margaret** Milton. She asked.
**Rebecca** Does Ray know? That you're loaded, I mean.
**Milton** I hope not. And I'd prefer it if ...
**Rebecca** Sure. I just wondered, that's all. He likes the smell of money, and he took a shine to you.
**Margaret** Perhaps he likes Milton for what he is. A pleasant enough man.
**Milton** Careful there, Margaret, with the hyperbole.
**Rebecca** It's just I know Ray's been tapping up anyone he thinks might have a bit put by — for that development he's planning down the coast. He showed me some drawings last night. You've gotta laugh. He plans to call it "Fisherman's Wharf"! What a joke.
**Margaret** That's progress, I suppose.
**Rebecca** But "Fisherman's Wharf", hello! It's an insult!
**Margaret** Oh, I don't know — that way, at least, folk won't forget what used to be.
**Rebecca** So now I've an idiot where once I had a mum.
**Milton** I don't think there's any need for that.
**Rebecca** What?
**Margaret** Milton?
**Milton** I'm sorry, I just don't think she should talk to her mother that way.
**Rebecca** Not your fucking business actually!
**Margaret** Rebecca!
**Rebecca** (*immediately regretting her behaviour*) OK. OK.
**Milton** It's fine. She's right.
**Margaret** No. She's rude. You're a guest in this house and we'd do well to remember our manners. Rebecca?

Act II, Scene 3                                                    37

**Rebecca**  I'm sorry, Milton. Really. I don't know where that came from.
**Milton**  I reckon I'll survive.
**Rebecca**  I'm an arse.
**Milton**  Accepted. (*Beat*) The apology, I mean.

*Rebecca goes and pours herself a glass of water and drinks. She realizes that, having created the atmosphere, it's up to her to break it*

**Rebecca**  So, OK, listen, Milt — did you bring any of these products over?
**Milton**  Well now, Rebecca — do I look like a skincare kind of guy?
**Rebecca**  I guess not ... but ... just to show?
**Milton**  To show to whom? For why?
**Rebecca**  To show *off*, I suppose, is what I meant.
**Milton**  I came here to escape. That meeting by the roadside was just a simple twist of fate. It meant that — at the grand old age of forty-five — I would never have to work again. Which, I know, makes me a lucky guy. But I don't feel any pride — it's just how things turned out. If you really want some lip balm, Rebecca, I'll be sure and send it on. Would you also like a baseball cap, a t-shirt, a washbag and a towel?
**Rebecca**  Hell, whatever, just package up the lot!
**Milton**  I'd far rather let you have a painting, to be honest.
**Rebecca**  OK.
**Margaret**  I'd like a painting, Milton ... of the sea.
**Milton**  Good choice, Margaret.
**Margaret**  I was teasing. But it would be nice to have a reminder.
**Rebecca**  Oh, I meant to say, Milt — if you need a lift to the station next week, let me know. I've a few trips to make. I can fit them around you, if you'd like.
**Milton**  That's kind, Rebecca, but I think I'd prefer it if your mother ...
**Margaret**  No, Milton, take the offer. I'm not much of a one for "goodbyes".
**Milton**  I'm only headed South — it's not as if I'm off and flying home.
**Margaret**  Let's not discuss it now. But Rebecca, there *is* something I wanted to say.
**Rebecca**  Go ahead.
**Margaret**  I just wanted to say, that despite your bad behaviour — I've quite enjoyed tonight. And I wouldn't mind if you came round for a meal regularly — if you liked. And perhaps — sometime — you might bring Pete.
**Rebecca**  (*after almost choking on her beer*) Pardon me?

*Milton smiles*

*Music*

*Black-out*

## Scene 4

*The coastal path. A few days later*

*The sound of seabirds. Milton takes photographs. Margaret is nearby*

*The music fades*

**Milton**  It's perfect. Today, it's almost perfect, don't you think?
**Margaret**  I'll take your word for it. It looks just the same to me. Honestly, Milton, how many pictures of the sea can one man need?
**Milton**  Oh, it's quite healthy, as obsessions go. I get fresh air and exercise, and nobody gets hurt. And besides — if I'm to do you a painting, Margaret — I wanna get it right.
**Margaret**  I'm sure I'll like it however it turns out.
**Milton**  That's not the point — *I* need to like it too. I need to think it's good enough for you. I won't be too long now.
**Margaret**  Take as long as you like. I'm fine just staring at the sea.
**Milton**  I was saying to Rebecca the other day — you can see the ocean from my place in Maine. Out the door, three minutes — you're on the beach. Some days I walk down there I don't see another soul. Thirty minutes walk up to the Point. That's a place — no matter what — always makes me feel it's *right* to be alive. In the other direction — ten minutes maybe — you get to the lake. Friend of mine has a little boat I borrow when the mood takes me. You ever take a boat out on a lake in the moonlight, Margaret? (*Pause*) On clear nights, the longer you look, the more stars seem to populate the sky. And the sounds. The wind whispering through the aspen leaves. The wailing of the loons. They're *birds* — they call to each other across the lake.
**Margaret**  It all sounds lovely, Milton.
**Milton**  It'd be so great to show you these things, Margaret — share them with you. I'm not asking for any guarantees. I've so much room and there's just me. I could set you up on the far side of the house — we could go entire days without having to meet. If you just came for a week or so — three at the most — you'd enjoy it so much, I just know. I just *know* you'd be sold ...

Act II, Scene 4                                                           39

**Margaret**  I can't just up and go halfway across the world — I've work to think of. And Rebecca, of course.
**Milton**  Rebecca has a life of her own. Face it, Margaret, those aren't reasons, they're excuses. I really can't see what you've got to lose. Don't you *ever* feel like just ... taking the plunge? Making that leap ... into the unknown?
**Margaret**  To be honest with you, no. And, by the way, I don't like feeling ... pressured.

*Silence*

You know, you're right.

*A brief moment of hope for Milton*

It does look different every day.
**Milton**  (*calmly*) The sea has many voices. Many gods and many voices.
**Margaret**  It's just you have to *concentrate*.

*Milton speaks out, as if to the sea, but his performance is for Margaret. He recites the first ten lines of Part IV of TS Eliot's "Four Quartets", Quartet No.3: "The Dry Salvages". His recitation is heartfelt; he loves those words and knows them well*

That was beautiful, Milton. Did you make it up?
**Milton**  Thomas Stearns Eliot — a fellow countryman. A true poet.
**Margaret**  I know who TS Eliot is. He wrote *Cats*.
**Milton**  In a manner of speaking. (*Beat*) You're pulling my leg, right? I'd get used to it, in the end, I guess.
**Margaret**  It all seems so easy to you. You're ... well-travelled, worldly. I feel tied. I've lived 'round here most my life — it's what I know. I may not always be content, but I'm comfortable.
**Milton**  Comfortable? Is that the most we can hope for? I think you deserve to be *happy*, Margaret, every single day. I mean it.
**Margaret**  I'm sure you do. It's just ... all too much. Too soon.
**Milton**  OK. Then how about a compromise: a long weekend down south. Come and stay with me for a few days before I leave — in a comfy Bed & Breakfast by the sea. No strings attached — we'll book you a room. How could that hurt? Just a couple of days ...
**Margaret**  Let it go, Milton. Please?
**Milton**  Fine. I give up. (*Pause*) But you should know: I didn't come looking for any of this. Nothing was further from my mind. But hey,

don't we have a duty to ourselves to build upon the good things that we find?
**Margaret**  I've enjoyed these past few weeks. Let's just leave it at that.
**Milton**  Look at me, Margaret. (*He takes her picture*) Now I'm done.

*Black-out*

*Music*

## Scene 5

*Margaret's kitchen. A few days later. Morning*

*Milton sits at the table putting his mobile number into Margaret's mobile phone. Margaret stands. Milton's stuff is all packed up ready to go. His coat is on the back of a chair*

*The music fades*

**Milton**  It's done. You just find "Milton" in the list, then press "phone". And when I call you, my name will come up on the screen.
**Margaret**  I know how it works, Milton, I'm not senile.
**Milton**  No, just resistant. Even so, we never got to have a proper argument, did we?
**Margaret**  I'm not much of a one for arguing. I'd rather sulk.
**Milton**  You know, sometimes I think you really don't like who you are. (*Pause*) And that's why you deprive yourself. It's a sort of self-inflicted punishment, right? (*Pause*) Your masochistic tendency, Margaret, is patently absurd.
**Margaret**  You won't bamboozle me into changing my mind, Milton.
**Milton**  Can I help it if you've become valuable to me? Goddammit, you *know* how I feel. And I think you feel the same. So why the hell deny it?
**Margaret**  Rebecca will be here soon. I should get ready. I'm due at work for nine.

*Margaret puts her coat on, checks her bag — does the sort of things she always does when she prepares to leave for work: unplugs stuff, closes drawers, puts lids on properly, repositions things. Milton is agitated — and as the scene progresses he becomes increasingly desperate. He will run both his hands back through his hair. Later, as he becomes more fraught, he may occasionally roll the heel of his hand on his trouser-leg — as if attempting to rub something away*

Act II, Scene 5                                                           41

**Milton**  OK, I couldn't tempt you with a week further down the coast. You've work, it was short notice — fine. But now I'll ask you one last time – to consider coming back to Maine with me. Just for a holiday at least. Please, Margaret, some time, you've gotta make up your mind to just ... try again ... to *be* again ... complete.
**Margaret**  Gobbledegook. You sound like Rebecca, when she started college — coming home with a head full of jargon. This is what I'm like — set in my ways; do you want to deal with that for the rest of your days? Maybe you're right, Milton — I don't like myself; but perhaps that's not something I can change. (*Pause*) You've upset me now. Lock up when you leave and give Rebecca the key. I know you feel I'm letting you down, Milton — and I'm sorry. (*Resolutely*) I shall give you a kiss and then I'll go. (*She kisses him swiftly, then starts to move towards the door*)
**Milton**  Is this really how you want it all to end?
**Margaret**  I told you I wasn't good at "goodbyes".
**Milton**  I want to stop you. (*He bangs his fist on the table*) I have to stop you.
**Margaret**  Don't be so ridiculous.
**Milton**  This is stupid. You're wrong. You're making a mistake. You won't see. Why don't you see? Why can't you realize? Why won't you accept the fact ... the fact ... the fact that whatever life has thrown at you, you're actually still ... you're actually still ... you're still ... alive ...
**Margaret**  (*confused by his behaviour*) For goodness' sake, Milton ...
**Milton**  ... You live and breathe. You have rights. You have ... needs. Hopes and. Hopes and. Hopes and. But, no. You won't see. Why won't you see? What's that about, Margaret? What is this? Are you being ... what is it ... are you being ... what? Deliberately obtuse?
**Margaret**  I don't know what you mean ...
**Milton**  There you go again, acting simple. Or is that a joke? Is that a joke, Margaret? Are you simply f ...? Are you f ...? Are you f ... (*He goes as if to stand, then collapses to the floor*)

*After a moment of confusion Margaret runs over to him.*

**Margaret**  What is it? Milton? Milton!? Please ... speak to me. Is it your heart?

*Milton starts to come round*

**Milton**  My heart is fine, Margaret. My heart is ... Candy. I need candy. In my coat. No, wait ... first — juice. Fridge. There's some left.

*Margaret goes to the fridge — brings out a half bottle of apple juice — hovers briefly, as if thinking to find a glass*

Bottle. Bottle!

*Margaret gives him the bottle. He drinks*

Candy. Coat.

*Milton knocks back the juice. Margaret goes to his coat. She rifles through the pockets, finding many empty and various sweet wrappers — finally amongst the wrappers she finds some Musketeers (or Milky Way) Funsize bars. She takes a handful to Milton. He is starting to recover*

**Margaret** Here.
**Milton** Thanks. (*He eats one*) You wanna try help me up?
**Margaret** Sure.

*Margaret helps Milton up to sit at the table. She piles up some bars beside him. He eats a couple more through the scene*

**Milton** They call these bars "Funsize". Better watch out, doll. The fun could start anytime.
**Margaret** You're diabetic.
**Milton** (*sarcastically*) You missed your vocation, Margaret.
**Margaret** What I *meant* was — you never said.
**Milton** It's not something I feel the need to share.
**Margaret** That's daft.
**Milton** Is it?
**Margaret** Yes.
**Milton** I stand corrected.
**Margaret** We make a fine pair.
**Milton** Do we?
**Margaret** The girl runs the bakery at the store, Miranda — she's a diabetic. You'll have seen her probably — pretty thing, red hair. You should look after yourself better.
**Milton** I'm fine. We caught it in time. I'll be OK now — honestly. Did I shout?
**Margaret** You weren't yourself.
**Milton** I shouted. I'm sorry. Whatever it was — I didn't mean it.
**Margaret** And I thought it was because you cared.
**Milton** Get to work.
**Margaret** I can wait for Rebecca. She'll be here in ten minutes.
**Milton** Don't make yourself late. It's not needed. I mean it.

Act II, Scene 6                                             43

**Margaret** Well, if you're sure.
**Milton** I absolutely insist.
**Margaret** OK, Milton. (*She kisses him on the forehead*) Be safe.

*Margaret goes to leave. She has reached the door when Milton calls to her. She stops, turns back — perhaps a little too eagerly*

**Milton** Margaret!
**Margaret** What is it?
**Milton** You forgot your cell.

*Margaret comes back, picks up her phone, pockets it — then heads out again. She turns back briefly at the door. She looks at Milton*

*Black-out*

*Music*

### Scene 6

*The same. One week later. Late at night*

*It's raining outside. Margaret and Rebecca have finished eating. The remains of a meal are on the table. There is an open newspaper in evidence on the sideboard, with the dictionary and encyclopaedia nearby. Margaret seems distracted at the beginning of this scene*

*The music fades*

**Margaret** You get on if you'd like, love, I'll do this. Didn't you say you'd an early start?

*Margaret takes the plates from the table to the sink then busies herself washing up, wiping surfaces etc.*

**Rebecca** The whole office is in chaos at the moment — they're just processing another batch of refugees. Pete's volunteered to help out — with the forms and stuff, if needs be. Some of them, of course, are better qualified than me. Not that you'd know that from what you read. What the poor sods must feel when they find they've fetched up here, I've no idea. (*Pause*) So they accepted his poem, anyway.
**Margaret** What's that?
**Rebecca** Pete's poem — the one he wrote to be put up on the train.

**Margaret** He'll be pleased.
**Rebecca** And Ray asked for a copy for the bar. He's gonna have it framed. Said he couldn't see why all this "culture" had to be confined to trains.
**Margaret** I saw Ray at the store the other day. He asked if I was wedded to my job. Said he's gonna be looking to recruit someone local to be Deputy Centre Manager down at Fisherman's Wharf. Not for a while of course yet, but still.
**Rebecca** He mentioned something about it the other night. I didn't want to get your hopes up.
**Margaret** I may not be cut out for it, of course. He said it'd be a "Liaison Operation" in the main. I'd just be expected to act in a "facilitative capacity" at first. I've got that off pat 'cos I wrote it down. (*Beat*) After he'd gone.
**Rebecca** So you've been "head-hunted", in a way.
**Margaret** Is that good?
**Rebecca** He wants someone reliable. Someone he can trust.
**Margaret** It might be too much. I know where I am up at the store. I don't want to overstretch myself.
**Rebecca** It'd be good for you.
**Margaret** Maybe I'll pop in and see him tomorrow night.
**Rebecca** We could join you for a drink, if you'd like — me *and* Pete, I mean. Oh, I brought you this. (*She takes a book out of her bag*) It's the anthology with Pete's poem in. He got ten complimentary copies. We know you don't like poetry, but he thought —
**Margaret** I'll look at it later.
**Rebecca** I've bookmarked the page. I really like it. It's about the trawlermen and their taboo words. It's called "The Things They Couldn't Say". I told him about the cards I made when I was little. Do you remember?
**Margaret** You insisted we go through them everyday.
**Rebecca** It was a long time ago.
**Margaret** I know. But even so ...
**Rebecca** Porpoise.
**Margaret** All right. Pig.
**Rebecca** Egg.
**Margaret** Wait a minute. Cat.
**Rebecca** Rat.
**Margaret** OK ... Clergyman!
**Rebecca** Devil.
**Margaret** And knife.
**Rebecca** Salmon.
**Margaret** Hare.
**Rebecca** Church.

**Margaret**  Dog.
**Rebecca**  Salt.
**Margaret**  Rabbit.

*Margaret sits at the table opposite Rebecca*

**Rebecca**  And ...
**Margaret**
**Rebecca**  } (*together*) Goodbye.

*Margaret is trying to stop herself from crying*

**Rebecca**  What is it?
**Margaret**  (*placing her hand on the poetry book*) He's good to you, isn't he?
**Rebecca**  Yes.
**Margaret**  I'm glad.
**Rebecca**  Mum, what's wrong?
**Margaret**  Your father and I ... we never really hit it off.
**Rebecca**  What's this about?
**Margaret**  It's been preying on my mind.
**Rebecca**  OK ...
**Margaret**  That's not to say he wouldn't have liked *you* — I'm sure he would. I was *fond* of him, of course I was. We led such sheltered lives. Oh, I don't know, Rebecca. Milton asked me to go away with him. To go back to his home. In Maine.
**Rebecca**  And what did you say?
**Margaret**  It took me by surprise. I didn't know what to do for the best. He seems fond of me. It's a bit ... frightening.
**Rebecca**  But what about you? Do you ... feel the same? Mum?
**Margaret**  I've never felt this way before.
**Rebecca**  And yet you let him just ... walk out the door?
**Margaret**  I don't know — it seemed ... I mean, at *our* age. I don't feel equipped ... to cope with all that stuff.
**Rebecca**  You mean "love"? Well, welcome to the club. None of us are. That's the risk. That's what it's all about.
**Margaret**  It's such a fuss ...
**Rebecca**  We're *all* afraid, Mum, you know. We just cover it up as best we can. We bumble about, we make idiots of ourselves. Isn't that why pop songs exist? To tell us it's OK to feel like this. Confused, fearful, gut-churningly insecure. I can't believe you've lived this long without finding this shit out. But it's today Milton leaves, right? Tonight he flies back home?

*Margaret gets up, fetches a bottle of wine from the fridge and a glass from the cupboard*

**Margaret**  He'll be at the airport, I suppose. I've left my phone on in case he bothers to call.
**Rebecca**  You could always call him, of course. (*Pause*) Mum?
**Margaret**  I've got the poetry book — and my bottle of wine.

*Margaret places the bottle and glass on the table*

**Rebecca**  Mum ...
**Margaret**  You know, love, if he doesn't call ... or send that painting like he promised — well, never mind. For a few weeks, at least, we were friends.

*Rebecca goes to her and hugs her. Margaret is slightly more responsive these days*

**Rebecca**  I'll call you in the morning.
**Margaret**  There's no need.
**Rebecca**  Perhaps I ought to stay.
**Margaret**  Really, love, I'd rather be by myself.
**Rebecca**  (*taking Margaret's hand*) Mum ...
**Margaret**  I'm sorry, Rebecca.
**Rebecca**  What for?
**Margaret**  (*patting Rebecca's hand*) Thanks, love.
**Rebecca**  What are you like?

*Rebecca hugs Margaret again, then takes her bag from the back of the chair. As she passes Margaret on her way to the door she takes her hand, briefly — then leaves*

*Music. Margaret pours herself some wine. She gets up and turns off the outside light and the main light. She sits back down, placing the book of poetry in front of her. She picks up her mobile phone from the sideboard, looks at it, then puts it down on the table beside the book. She's now lit only by the light on the sideboard. She takes a sip of wine*

*The music fades*

*The rain gets louder*

## Scene 7

*Night*

*Milton is standing in the rain. Pale moonlight. We should have no idea where he is. We hear the sound of a Boeing C-17 Globemaster III flying over. As the sound fades Milton starts to speak*

**Milton**  In nineteen-eleven Franklin Bowden Broome suddenly upped sticks and headed South. In later documentation, rumours of a sex scandal emerged — hints of a tryst with a sea captain's wife — but no evidence for this ever came to light. Twenty years ago an unseen work — a rough watercolour — was discovered in a sketchbook in a publisher's attic in Portland, Maine. This work, inelegantly titled: "A Fine Bright Day Today" — was later used as the cover design for a popular novel. It sold nine million copies round the globe. Bowden Broome's art had finally reached a world-wide market. Five years ago Sotheby's sold that sketchbook for one hundred thousand dollars. To me. (*Pause*) Just as a singular event — a tragic loss, or a chance meeting – might shape or define a person's life — it is the way this under-appreciated artist met his end (rather than his work) that has ensured the name Franklin Bowden Broome lives on today. After a six month sojourn in the West Country, he left these shores — sailing out of Southampton on the tenth of April nineteen-twelve, bound for New York. He never made it home. In the early hours of the fifteenth of April, when the ship went down, over fifteen hundred people were drowned. Along with almost twelve hundred other souls — Franklin Bowden Broome was lost at sea.

*Milton takes out his mobile phone, makes a call. Margaret's phone begins to ring. She answers it*

**Margaret**  Hello.
**Milton**  Margaret. It's Milton.
**Margaret**  I know. Your name came up. I hoped you'd call before you left. Are you at the airport?
**Milton**  I'm outside. I don't suppose you'd let me in. I'm rather wet.

*Black-out*

*Music*

## Scene 8

*Margaret's kitchen. A few moments later*

*Milton enters. Margaret follows. She helps him out of his wet coat*

*Music fades*

**Milton** I seem to be dripping on your floor.
**Margaret** Let's hope you haven't caught pneumonia. Shall I make you a hot drink?
**Milton** No, really, Margaret, I'm fine. Just tired.
**Margaret** So what happened to your flight?
**Milton** It probably went without me, don't you think? (*Pause*) I got a taxi to the bottom of the hill, then walked up. I didn't want to wake you. I've been stood outside thinking things through. I thought you might be angry. Then it struck me — what the hell! Of course I'd no idea your phone would actually be on ...
**Margaret** I'm glad to see you, Milton. But you do look exhausted. I was about to turn in.
**Milton** Fine. How about we see how the land lies in the morning? I'm assuming it's all right for me to stay?
**Margaret** I'm hardly gonna turn you away.
**Milton** Great.
**Margaret** Oh, I've stripped your bed, I'm afraid.
**Milton** Of course ——
**Margaret** But you can come in with me. If you don't mind.
**Milton** Well, I ——

*Margaret kisses him. It becomes a passionate kiss. Margaret breaks away and heads towards the stairs. Milton is rooted to the spot. Margaret turns back towards him, waits*

**Margaret** You fit then?
**Milton** Oh. Sure ...
**Margaret** Well, hurry up. You've already kept me waiting half the night.

*Milton goes over towards the stairs*

Oh, I almost forgot. You go on up.

*Milton goes upstairs*

Act II, Scene 8

*Margaret comes back and turns the light on the sideboard off*

**Margaret** That's not like me at all.

*Now the kitchen is lit by the moonlight through the window and the light flooding down the stairs*

   *Margaret heads off upstairs*

*After a moment the landing light snaps out. The moonlight slowly fades*

*Black-out*

# FURNITURE AND PROPERTY LIST

## ACT I

### Scene 1

*On stage*:  Table. *On it*: crossword puzzle, dictionary, encyclopaedia
Chairs
Sketch book (for **Milton**)
Biscuit jar containing biscuits
Sink
Kettle
Fridge containing milk, beer, yoghurt, wine and apple juice
Cupboard containing plates
Sideboard with drawers containing bottle opener and cutlery
Hook on wall
Mirror
Tray
Teapot
Cups
Jar
Glasses
Toaster
Cafetière

*Off stage*:  Box of books (**Rebecca**)
Box (**Rebecca**)
Bin bag full of stuff (**Rebecca**)

*Personal*:  **Milton**: sweet bars, empty wrappers (in pocket of coat)

### Scene 2

*Set*:  Framed picture

*Off stage*:  Box of junk including candleholder, envelope of photographs, hideous old wall-plate, old vase and old books (**Margaret**)

### Scene 3

*Set*:  Flowers
Pile of old newspapers

Furniture and Property List

*Off stage*:  Bucket (**Margaret**)

## Scene 4

*On stage*:  As before

*Off stage*:  Camera bag, artist's case (**Rebecca**)
Huge back-pack (**Milton**)
Bags of shopping including bottle of wine (**Margaret**)

## Scene 5

*Set*:  Bread
Pan for eggs
Scrambled eggs

## Scene 6

*Strike*:  Breakfast things

*Set*:  Camera (for **Milton**)

## Scene 7

*Strike*:  Camera

*Set*:  Remains of a meal
Bread
Empty wine bottle

# ACT II

## Scene 1

*Strike*:  Remains of meal
Bread
Empty wine bottle

*Set*:  Pills

## Scene 2

*Set*:  Camera on tripod

|  |  |
|---|---|
|  | Sketch book |

### Scene 3

|  |  |
|---|---|
| *Strike*: | Camera |
|  | Sketch book |
| *Set*: | Debris from a meal |

### Scene 4

|  |  |
|---|---|
| *Set*: | Camera |

### Scene 5

|  |  |
|---|---|
| *Set*: | **Margaret**'s mobile phone |
|  | **Milton**'s backpack and belongings |

### Scene 6

|  |  |
|---|---|
| *Strike*: | **Milton**'s belongings |
| *Set*: | Remains of a meal |
|  | Bag containing book (for **Rebecca**) |
| *Check*: | Open newspaper |

### Scene 7

|  |  |
|---|---|
| *On stage*: | As before |
| *Personal*: | **Milton**: mobile phone |

### Scene 8

|  |  |
|---|---|
| *On stage*: | As before |

# LIGHTING PLOT

Practical fittings required: table lamp

ACT I, SCENE 1

*To open*: Interior lighting on kitchen

| | | |
|---|---|---|
| *Cue* 1 | Sound of seabirds<br>*Bring up lights on* **Milton** *on cliff path* | (Page 1) |
| *Cue* 2 | **Milton**: "... I think I made a friend."<br>*Fade lights on* **Milton** | (Page 3) |
| *Cue* 3 | **Margaret** exits<br>*Fade lights on kitchen. Bring up lights on* **Milton** | (Page 4) |
| *Cue* 4 | Music<br>*Black-out* | (Page 5) |

ACT I, SCENE 2

*To open*: Interior lighting on kitchen

| | | |
|---|---|---|
| *Cue* 5 | Music<br>*Black-out* | (Page 8) |

ACT I, SCENE 3

*To open*: Interior lighting on kitchen

| | | |
|---|---|---|
| *Cue* 6 | Music<br>*Black-out* | |

ACT I, SCENE 4

*To open*: Kitchen in darkness with some light filtering through from outside

| | | |
|---|---|---|
| *Cue* 7 | **Rebecca** turns on lights<br>*Bring up lights on kitchen* | (Page 12) |
| *Cue* 8 | **Margaret** turns on the table lamp<br>*Snap off light filtering through from outside* | (Page 15) |

| | | |
|---|---|---|
| *Cue* 9 | **Margaret** turns on outside light<br>*Snap on light filtering through from outside* | (Page 17) |
| *Cue* 10 | **Margaret** turns off main light<br>*Snap off lighting on kitchen* | (Page 17) |
| *Cue* 11 | Music<br>*Black-out* | (Page 17) |

ACT I, SCENE 5

*To open*: Exterior lighting on **Milton**, sunrise

| | | |
|---|---|---|
| *Cue* 12 | **Milton**: " — only disappointment lies."<br>*Bring up lights on kitchen* | (Page 17) |
| *Cue* 13 | Music plays<br>*Black-out* | (Page 20) |

ACT I, SCENE 6

*To open*: Exterior lighting

| | | |
|---|---|---|
| *Cue* 14 | **Milton**: "It looks like rain."<br>*Black-out* | (Page 23) |

ACT I, SCENE 7

*To open*: Interior lighting on kitchen

| | | |
|---|---|---|
| *Cue* 15 | **Milton**: "Everything's just fine."<br>*Black-out* | (Page 29) |

ACT II, SCENE 1

*To open*: Exterior lighting on **Milton**, interior lighting on kitchen

| | | |
|---|---|---|
| *Cue* 16 | Music<br>*Black-out* | (Page 31) |

ACT II, SCENE 2

*To open*: Exterior lighting

| | | |
|---|---|---|
| *Cue* 17 | Music<br>*Black-out* | (Page 33) |

Lighting Plot

ACT II, SCENE 3

*To open*: Interior lighting on kitchen

*Cue* 18  Music  (Page 38)
          *Black-out*

ACT II, SCENE 4

*To open*: Exterior lighting

*Cue* 19  **Milton**: "Now I'm done."  (Page 40)
          *Black-out*

ACT II, SCENE 5

*To open*: Interior lighting on kitchen

*Cue* 20  **Margaret** turns back at the door and looks at **Milton**  (Page 43)
          *Black-out*

ACT II, SCENE 6

*To open*: Interior lighting on kitchen, light filtering in from outside. Practical on with covering spot

*Cue* 21  **Margaret** turns off outside light and main light  (Page 46)
          *Snap off outside light and interior lighting*

ACT II, SCENE 7

*To open*: Pale moonlight

*Cue* 22  **Milton**: "I'm rather wet."  (Page 47)
          *Black-out*

ACT II, SCENE 8

*To open*: Practical on with covering spot. Moonlight filtering in from outside.

*Cue* 22  **Milton** goes upstairs  (Page 48)
          *Snap on light flooding down stairs*

*Cue* 23  **Margaret** goes upstairs  (Page 49)
          *After a moment, snap off light flooding down stairs.*
          *Fade moonlight slowly to black-out*

# EFFECTS PLOT

ACT I

| | | |
|---|---|---|
| Cue 1 | To open SCENE 1<br>*Music* | (Page 1) |
| Cue 2 | **Margaret** peeps out the window<br>*Bump from upstairs* | (Page 1) |
| Cue 3 | **Margaret** leafs through a dictionary<br>*Sound of someone coming downstairs* | (Page 1) |
| Cue 4 | **Margaret** looks up<br>*Sound of seabirds. Music fades* | (Page 1) |
| Cue 5 | **Rebecca** "I'm fine."<br>*Jet-fighter flies low overhead* | (Page 2) |
| Cue 6 | **Margaret** looks after **Rebecca**<br>*Sound of truck door slamming and truck moving off* | (Page 4) |
| Cue 7 | **Milton** starts to eat a sweet bar<br>*Music* | (Page 5) |
| Cue 8 | To open SCENE 2<br>*Music fades. Sound of pick-up truck drawing up* | (Page 5) |
| Cue 9 | **Rebecca** exits<br>*Music* | (Page 8) |
| Cue 10 | To open SCENE 3<br>*Fade music. Sound of rain* | (Page 8) |
| Cue 11 | **Milton**: "You got me there."<br>*Music* | (Page 12) |
| Cue 12 | To open SCENE 4<br>*Sound of pick-up drawing up outside* | (Page 12) |
| Cue 13 | **Rebecca** and **Milton** enter<br>*Music fades* | (Page 12) |

Effects Plot

| | | |
|---|---|---|
| *Cue* 14 | **Milton** leaves<br>*Sound of pick-up starting up and driving away* | (Page 16) |
| *Cue* 15 | **Margaret** struggles off upstairs<br>*Music* | (Page 17) |
| *Cue* 16 | To open Scene 5<br>*Music fades* | (Page 17) |
| *Cue* 17 | **Margaret** looks at **Milton** and smiles<br>*Music* | (Page 20) |
| *Cue* 18 | To open Scene 6<br>*Sound of seabirds. Music fades* | |
| *Cue* 19 | **Margaret**: "... riskier way to make a living."<br>*Jet fighter flies over, very low* | (Page 21) |
| *Cue* 20 | Black-out<br>*Music* | (Page 23) |
| *Cue* 21 | To open Scene 7<br>*Music fades* | (Page 23) |
| *Cue* 22 | **Margaret**: "... how high you set your standards."<br>*Sound of car drawing up outside* | (Page 24) |
| *Cue* 23 | **Milton**: " ... and to Ray."<br>*Sound of car driving off* | (Page 26) |

ACT II

| | | |
|---|---|---|
| *Cue* 24 | To open Scene 1<br>*Music plays, then fades* | (Page 30) |
| *Cue* 25 | **Margaret** puts her head in her hands<br>*Music* | (Page 31) |
| *Cue* 26 | To open Scene 2<br>*Sound of seabirds. Music fades* | (Page 32) |
| *Cue* 27 | **Milton**: "Is that so?"<br>*A jet-fighter hurtles by overhead* | (Page 32) |
| *Cue* 28 | **Milton** starts to eat a sweet<br>*Music* | (Page 33) |

| | | |
|---|---|---|
| *Cue* 29 | **Rebecca** fetches a beer from the fridge<br>*Music fades* | (Page 34) |
| *Cue* 30 | **Milton** smiles<br>*Music* | (Page 38) |
| *Cue* 31 | To open Scene 4<br>*Sound of seabirds. Music fades* | (Page 38) |
| *Cue* 32 | Black-out<br>*Music* | (Page 40) |
| *Cue* 33 | To open Scene 5<br>*Music fades* | (Page 40) |
| *Cue* 34 | Black-out<br>*Music* | (Page 43) |
| *Cue* 35 | To open Scene 6<br>*Rain. Music fades* | (Page 43) |
| *Cue* 36 | **Rebecca** leaves<br>*Music* | (Page 46) |
| *Cue* 37 | **Margaret** takes a sip of wine<br>*Music fades. Rain gets louder* | (Page 46) |
| *Cue* 38 | To open Scene 7<br>*Sound of Boeing C-17 Globemaster III flying over* | (Page 47) |
| *Cue* 39 | **Milton** makes a call on his phone<br>**Margaret**'s *phone begins to ring* | (Page 47) |
| *Cue* 40 | Black-out<br>*Music* | (Page 47) |
| *Cue* 41 | To open Scene 8<br>*Music fades* | (Page 48) |

USE OF COPYRIGHT MUSIC

A licence issued by Samuel French Ltd to perform this play does not include permission to use any Incidental music specified in this copy. Where the place of performance is already licensed by the PERFORMING RIGHT SOCIETY a return of the music used must be made to them. If the place of performance is not so licensed then application should be made to the Performing Right Society, 29 Berners Street, London W1T 3AB.

A separate and additional licence from PHONOGRAPHIC PERFORMANCES LTD, 1 Upper James Street, London W1R 3HG is needed whenever commercial recordings are used.

www.ingramcontent.com/pod-product-compliance
Ingram Content Group UK Ltd.
Pitfield, Milton Keynes, MK11 3LW, UK
UKHW021847210426
5322IPUK00022B/513